THE SECRET POWER WITHIN

DR. GEORGE D. HAMILTON

Library of congress cataloging-in- Publication Data George D. Hamilton, D.D., Th.D.

The Secret Power Within

Registered with Copyright Office Library of Congress – copyright © pending. Copyright © 2010 by George D. Hamilton.

Unless otherwise indicated scripture quotations in this book are from The King James Version of the Holy Bible.

Library of Congress Catalog Card Number

ISBN 978-1530459445

MY DAILY AFFIRMATION

I AM A SPIRIT.

I HAVE A SOUL.

AND I LIVE IN A BODY.

RECONIZING MY TRUE IDENITY

PREFACE

Suppose someone asked you to name the **Master Secret** of the ages. What would you answer? Atomic Energy? Interplanetary Travel? Black Holes? No, it is not any of these. Then what is this **Master Secret?** Where can one find it? How can it be understood and put into action? The answer is extraordinarily simple. This secret is the marvelous, miracle-working power found in your own Human Spirit (the real you). This is the last place most people would look for it.

THIS BOOK WILL HELP YOU FIND THIS SECRET!

THE TRIUNE HOMO SAPIEN

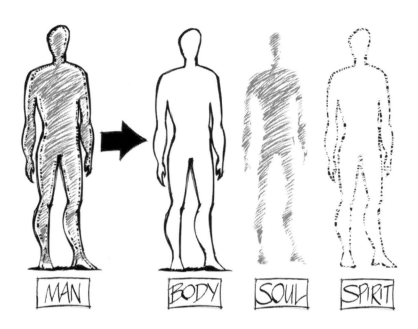

CONTENTS

THIS BOOK IS YOUR KEY TO:

INTRODUCTION

"This is the day which the Lord hath made; we will rejoice and be glad in it." Psalm 118:24

Live victoriously 365 days a year! Is it really possible? It is not only possible, but this blessing has also been promised to every believer who will appropriate it by faith. Jesus came to give us an abundant life – free from sin, sickness, worry, poverty, depression, fear, frustration, and defeat. Most Christians, however, have allowed Satan, who is described by Jesus as a thief (John 10:10), to rob them of their health and prosperity, as well as usurp their rights and authority. Did you know that God never intended that His children should be sick and afflicted, nor poverty stricken and oppressed? Are you aware that it is His will for you to prosper, and be in health, even as your soul prospers (3 John 2)? Did you know that He desires for you to live a fruitful and abundant life, walking in victory 365 days a year? God has pledged that His children, who obey His Word, shall enjoy prosperity in all things: *"And he shall be like a tree planted by the rivers of water, that bringeth forth his fruit in his season; his leaf also shall not wither; and whatsoever doeth shall prosper" (Psalm 1:3)*. We are not suggesting that God intended that His children should live a life free from any

1

problems or trials, or without testing, but we are suggesting that God has provided the means whereby these things will not be able to dominate us, as they do so many, and that they can be controlled and overcome. Most Christians have been reading the Bible for years, and it seems it has never occurred to them that God has invited them to walk through life on a pathway literally paved with His promises. There are thousands of promises in the Word of God made to the believer, and yet the average Christian has appropriated but one of the promise of salvation in John 3:16. A certain number have, to be sure, claimed the promise of the baptism in the Holy Spirit (Luke 11:13), and others, the promise of divine healing (Mark 16:18), but few Christians have grasped the full nature of their inheritance as joint-heirs with Christ. The Scriptures are filled with divine assurances, rights, privileges, blessings, and promises, given to us, whereby God has made provision for our every spiritual, physical, and temporal need, as well as for the accomplishment of the work He has commissioned His Church to do. All these provisions and blessings are available to the extent that we are willing to press through by faith and appropriate them. Jesus characterizes Satan as a thief who has come to rob you of your abundant life and defeat you through circumstances. The Enemy has most Christians deceived into believing that all of the promises of temporal blessing are for the past, applying only to Israel, and the promises of spiritual blessing are for the future, in heaven, in spite of such glorious promises as are found, for example, in

Matthew 6:19-34; Mark 11:22-24; 16:16-20; Luke 11:13; I Corinthians 3:21-22; Philippians 4:19; John 2. The Word of God promises the believer an abundant and fruitful life, with the assurance that by faith and understand the Human Spirit and spiritual laws he can rise above all opposing circumstances. Also, endure even the severest trials, overcome his problems, enjoy peace and security, and walk in victory 365 days a year. For most Christians, however, life consists in just getting by somehow day by day – hoping they will not get sick – worried as to whether or not the money will hold out until the end of the month – praying that children will not get into serious trouble – hoping the old car will last through the winter – struggling to get through one more day, then catching a few hours' rest before beginning the endless cycle all over again tomorrow. Life consists of 365 days of cares, worries, and problems, with only an occasional ray of sunshine breaking through the dark clouds of life. This mediocre form of living is definitely not God's Will for His children, and results from the fact that, although most Christians have been taught how to prepare for death, few have learned how to live. Thus, one day looks like the next to them, occupied with cares, problems, troubles, and worries. Life has become, for most it seems, sheer drudgery. Let me ask you some questions. How were your last 365 days of life as a Christian? Were they filled with joy, victory, and accomplishment? Were you able to overcome your problems? Did you endure your trials in faith? Was there a definite growth

3

in your spiritual life? Did you experience an increase in your faith? Or were your last 365 days not much different from those of Mr. and Mrs. Average Christian – occupied with cares troubles, sickness, disappointments, and failures. Did you know that God has set forth in His Word certain kingdom principles concerning our thoughts, attitudes, and our confession that will enable the Christian to achieve emotional stability, and peace of mind, as well as an enduring faith, which will empower him to walk in victory over all circumstances each day? This is no empty hope, impossible of realization, but is more and more becoming the actual experience of many saints, who, because of their uncompromising faith in the Word of God, are, as the Psalmist describes them, like a tree planted by the rivers of water, who bring forth their fruit in its season, whose leaf also does not wither, and whatsoever they do prospers. What is the secret of such victorious living? Apostle John said, *"For whatsoever is born of God overcometh the world..." (1 John 5:4)*. We have been created in the image of God and given the key to the secret of life. We are spirit with supernatural power to control our world. This book will teach you how to tap into the secret power that lies within you. This God given power will enable you to live a victorious life 365 days a year.

CHAPTER ONE

THE LAW AND DEFINITION OF FAITH

The word faith is found only twice in the Old Testament, but 245 times in the New Testament. The word believe with its various ending occurs 45 times in the Old Testament and 268 times in the New Testament. The word *Trust* is another Old Testament word for *Faith* and *Belief*. It is used with its various endings 154 times in the Old Testament and 35 times in the New Testament. These words simply mean to confide in, so as to be secure without fear; to flee for refuge to or to take shelter in; to put faith in; to stay or rest on; rely on; to believe or to take at his word; to rely upon the promise of another; and to put absolute trust in a person without any questioning or doubts as to His faithfulness. The Bible definition of faith is, *"Now faith the substance of things hoped for, the evidence of things not seen" (Heb. 11:1).* Various renderings express this verse thus: *"Now faith is a well- grounded assurance of that for which we hope, and a conviction of the reality of things which we do not see."* (Weymouth); *"Now faith means we are confident of what we hope for, convinced of what we do not see"* (Moffat); *"Now faith is the title- deed of things hoped for; the putting to proof of the things not seen"* (Centenary Translation) ; *"Now faith is an assumption of what is being expected, a conviction concerning matters which are not being observed"* (Concordant Version) ; *"Now faith is the persuasion of things that are in hope, as if they were in act; and it is the manifestness of things not seen."* NOW FAITH IS THE FOUNDATION OF THINGS HOPED FOR. Paul in Rom. 4:17 expresses true faith as an attribute of God, "who quickeneth the dead, and calleth those things which be not as though they were." Faith is a union of assurance and conviction, the counting or reckoning a thing done as though it were already done. Faith does not have to see before it believes. It laughs at impossibilities and all circumstances that may be contrary to it and counts the things done that it asks from God. Faith is not swayed to believe God only when things seem possible, and it is not moved to waver or question in the least when things seems to go contrary to what has been asked. It doggedly plugs right along counting the impossible as possible, counting as done the things that are not seen, and counting the things that are not as though they were.

WHAT IS FAITH?

It is the confident assurance that something we want is going to happen. It is the certainty that what we hope for is waiting for us, even though we cannot see it up ahead. Said another way, faith is the title deed to things we can't see. When we buy property, we meet with the sellers and papers are drawn up. We receive a deed and it says we own a stated piece of property. The minute it is signed, we own the property. We don't have to go to it; we don't have to see it. It's ours. We have a title deed. The same with faith. We have a title deed to what God has promised. Our role is to believe in our hearts that it has been accomplished, according to what God has given us the deed to, and then to speak it. We can't force it. We can't sit around a room with a group and work it up. We can receive it only from God. The bible says: *"So then faith cometh by hearing, and hearing by the word of God. (Rom.10:17).* We hear the Lord's Word; it builds in our hearts, and the light goes on. "It's mine!" Deep down inside, there will be no doubt. That is what the Lord meant when He referred in the fig tree episode to the one who speaks to the mountain and "does not doubt in his heart" the mountain will move. The Bible also cautions about double – mindedness: . .let him ask in faith without any doubts is like the surf of the sea driven and tossed by the wind. For let not that man expect that he will receive anything from the Lord, being a double minded man, unstable in all his ways. (James1:6-8) There can be no equivocating, no going back and forth. So many of us hear some- thing from the Lord, we believe it briefly, but the wind blows and the storm pounds and our faith in what God said vanishes like the mist. We need to counter by speaking the word God has given and then simply accepting it. I must add a word, however, to drive home a subtle point. Our faith throughout all of this must be in the Lord— "having faith in God," Jesus said—and not in our ability, our stubborn strength. Our faith is not to be in our faith: *"Trust in the Lord with all thine heart; and lean not unto thine own understanding." (Prov.3:5).* For the Lord, while structuring most of His dealing with man around the point of faith made plain that His insistence on faith was not quantitative, but qualitative. He said we would move mountain if we had faith the size of a mustard seed. We don't need a mountain of faith to move a mountain of dirt or even a mountain of world problems. The object and reality of the faith are the issues. We don't need stubbornness, but confidence. .... *"And this is the confidence that we have in him, that if we ask any thing according to his will, he heareth us. And if we know that he hears us, whatsoever we ask, we know that we have the petitions that we desired of him." (1 John 5:14-15)* Man's nature is two-fold. There is an inward man. The inward man is the spirit. The out- ward man is the Body. To believe with the heart means to believe on the inside, with the inward man. To base one's faith on physical evidence is to believe only from the natural human standpoint—to believe with the outward man. Real faith in God – Heart faith believes the Word of God regardless of what the physical evidence may be. Believing with the inward man that causes it to be manifested on the outside of them before they will believe on the inside and it doesn't work that way. These folks are letting their bodies--their physical senses—dominate them. They believe what the outward man, their physical body, tells them rather than what God's Word says. They are believing the truth of the natural rather than the truth of God's Word. A person seeking healing should look to God's Word, not to his symptoms. He should say, "I know that I am healed because the Word says that by His stripes I am healed." It wouldn't do any good just to say that unless you believed it in your heart, however, because it wouldn't work. But if you believe it with your heart and say it with your mouth, it will work. *"...Whosoever shall say unto this mountain...and shall not doubt in his heart, but shall believe those things which he saith shall come to pass; he shall have whatsoever he saith."(Mark 11:23)*

KEY SCRIPTURE READING

"For verily I say unto you, That whosoever shall say unto the mountain, be thou removed, and be thou cast into the sea: and shall not doubt in his heart, but shall believe that those things which he saith shall come to pass; he shall have whatsoever he saith." Mark 11:23

Therefore I say unto you, what things soever ye desire, when ye pray, believe that ye receive them, and ye shall have them."
Mark 11:24

CHAPTER TWO

UNVEILING THE LAW AND SECRET OF LIFE

The secret of life lies within each of us. This book will teach you how to tap into this secret to bring joy, happiness, peace, healing and prosperity into your personal life. It will teach you how to take control over the circumstances of your life and bring victory and success into your finances and healing into your body. On New Year's Eve many of us declare our resolutions, and most of us will have broken that commitment by New Year's Day. Why? Because we never actually believe we have what it takes to succeed. We expect some mysterious magical force will change us, and we will be able to keep our promises to ourselves. The truth is, we have the power within us to make our dreams come true. All we need to do is change the way we think. It is that simple. Instead of expecting life to be a struggle, money to be scarce, and people to be difficult, work to be dull, believe you can change your life – and it will. There is no mystery to it but, as a former colleague of mine used to say, "You've gotta wanna." That is the key. Desire is the fastest route to the rest of your life. The spirit and enthusiasm that is part of the divine nature (new birth) in all of us truly makes things happen. Change your thoughts and you change your world. Each day we are given opportunities to create a new life. God puts before us each day a challenge to change and choose a better life. In Deuteronomy 30:19 God says, *"I call heaven and earth to record this day against you, that I have set before you life and death, blessing and cursing: therefore choose life, that both thou and thy seed may live:"* With ever sunrise, God gives us new possibilities, options, and people to help shape our future. It is what we do with these gifts and how we feel about them that determines the quality of our lives. Seeing your life differently may be hard to master, but there is no in-between with this one. You change or you do not. That dictates your future. Change is scary. To have everything you ever wanted, you need to change the way you see things, especially the way you see life. We resist change in our lives. We resist committing to our future and the responsibility we share in shaping it. The power to live the life of our dreams and to draw all the things we need and want into our world comes from within our own consciousness. It is not outside of us. There is no energy acting upon us from some lofty place in the Universe. Our earthly, logical mind works together with the part of our consciousness that is God to shape the reality of our lives. The responsibility is ours and ours alone. If you want more from life, you need to do something about it. If you do not, no force will do it for you. Understanding your own hidden creative power is essential to your success in getting what you want. Here are some insights to help you realize that you must change your attitude to accomplish your goals. Read them, understand that they are true, and absorb their message.

THE LAW OF BELIEF

Belief is the most crucial key to success in manifesting your wants. And you don't even have to be that strong a believer either. That sounds strange but the Human Spirit hears your intention the minute you put it in motion. All you have to do is believe it's possible that you can get it. That's it! That single glimmer of hope is enough to change your world. Even when you think you have lost of hope or act out of despair, you're actually not despairing at all because you are trying to find a way to make things happen for yourself. For instances, you may find yourself at a time in your life when you are severely depressed, and you think that you have to get help or you will do yourself harm (Suicide). You ask your pastor for counseling and possible deliverance. You see, you are not really in despair because if you were, you would not have made an appointment with your pastor for counseling. That's my point. Part of you believes you can get better. This is belief in the truest and simplest form. And it's all anyone needs to accomplish great things. What if I can't get over my fear? Will I still be able to have the life I want? Eliminating fear is tough, but doable. It's not possible for us to eliminate all of our fears at once, but we can certainly get them under control so they don't get in the way of achieving our goals. Our minds don't have room for anything else. Fear is automatically eliminated faith and courage. Even though God has not given us a spirit of fear, most Christians allow themselves to get trapped in this negative emotional condition. Normal fears are everyday fare for most Christian. They are our insecurities about having enough money to pay the bills, or losing the little that we possess. It's the abnormal fears that stop us. They can be deep-seated fears of inadequacy, success or failure. Some of us are even afraid that we will always be afraid?

WHAT HAPPENS IF I DON'T REALLY KNOW WHAT I WANT?

Ah, this is a dilemma of infinite proportion! It's the age-old question arising all over again: "Why am I here?" It's very important to focus on what you want. If you don't know yet, the information in this book will help you to do this and decide upon your own unique need and wants, and how to get them 365 days a year. Now that you have an idea of what is motivating you and who you are, as you approach your future let's move ahead to identifying specific wants and desires.

DECIDE TO DECIDE

There are times when the only really comfortable decision we are able to make is what to have for dinner. There are so many choices available to us in this day and age that life becomes overwhelming and options seem endless. That leaves most of us confused. We know there are goals we have to achieve in this lifetime, before the rapture of the church and, there are places we would like to go. People we like to attract in our lives, the millions of dollars that we would like to have available to spend as we fit, cars, houses, vacation foreign countries etc. And yet it all seems untouchable. With so much out there, how can we truly know what we want? Just remember that the power to have everything you ever wanted lies in your own hands, but first you must decide to do it. Once that's done, the rest is a piece of cake.

IT'S YOUR TURN

The time has come for you to grab the reins and gallop forward. Decide to focus on the rest of your life and start right now. Take a look at the possibilities available to you. Assess what you can accomplish right now. Look to what you can make possible in this moment in time. But you are saying, "What about long terms goals? Isn't it good to look ahead?" I am not suggesting that you walk around with blinders on, but I am suggesting that you begin now and not put off until tomorrow, because there are no guarantees. Before you know it, tomorrow is here and you are into regret and self- admonition for not going for it when you had the chance. Take it from me, if I had not told myself that time was of the essence, you wouldn't be reading this book today, because it would still be a figment of my imagination and my desire. I can still hear you saying, "How? How do I get to the point where I decide what it is I want?" Here's how:

15

LOOK BACK ON YOUR LIFE, SO FAR, WITH LOVE

Knowing that you did the best you could, under the circumstances. Look at your past. Try to identify how you handled certain situations that did not work out as you hoped. Decide what you could do differently, or better, if the situation happened again today. Now mind you I am not telling you to try and change the past, but rather to use it as research in creating your future.

FORGIVE YOURSELF AND OTHERS FOR NOT GETTING EVERYTHING YOU WANTED OR NEEDED IN THE PAST.

That includes forgiving yourself first. Let go of the old you and say hello to the new you. Thank the old you for helping you to get to this point, and send her on her way. It also means forgiving those people whom you might have blamed for your troubles, like your parents, unfaithful friends, children, lovers, ex-wives, ex- husbands and so on. You get the idea. Know that they came into your life for a reason that is beyond the understanding of your conscious mind. They came in their strange and sometimes painful way, to teach you and to help you grow spiritually into the wonderful person you deserve to be. They were gifts from God to help you get closer to your divine calling. As the old saying goes "God works in mysterious ways."

DON'T BE ATTACHED TO THE RESULTS

This simply means that you should not worry about how things will turn out. Know that no matter what happens, there is a divine (Pre-ordained) plan in action. Trust in the power that is within you to lead you to the right place at the right time. You must trust that you will always get exactly what you should have for your spiritual growth, at this particular time in your life.

EMBRACE YOUR POWER

In my teaching on KINGDOM PRINCIPAL I have found that the hardest thing for people to do is to accept their greatness. Our mothers taught us as children not to be proud conceited or to toot our own horn, and frankly, we have taken these les- sons a bit too far. It's one thing to let our ego get the best of us, but it's another thing to deny the God-like power within us. We can recognize and accept that we have the power to make our dreams come true if we believe that we are created in the image of God (an exact expression of God's substance) with power to pro-create. If we truly understand that we are made of the same stuff as the earth, tree, and lower animals, we would better appreciate the power within (Human Spirit) us and the authority God gave mankind to exercise dominion (Genesis 1:26-27) over planet earth. Look around you and accept your place in the world (universe) and know that you have all of it to support you in whatever you decide to do. Connect with the power within;

that's connecting with the source that can help you (pro-create) achieve and attain everything you ever wanted. Make that connection and welcome the help that's so readily available to you. Accept how God has created you, and know that the power within (spirit) is the part of you that can climb mountains. There is nothing that can stop you. It's not enough to accept the power and greatness of your Human Spirit as the wind beneath your wings, so to speak, because there's more to do. The world (universe) relates to you as you, an individual source of power within a limitless energy field called life. The key here is accepting who and what you are, right here, right now, and leading from your strengths. Recognize what you do well and what you don't do well. Embrace all of you. Say to yourself, I am okay. I can do some things really well, and other things I can improve on or get help with. When you admit this, you accept your humanness instead of feeling sorry for your- self, and then go get moving toward your goal.

A QUESTION OF FAITH

But you say I am riddled with self-doubt. I have no self-esteem, and I really can't do anything well. In fact, I have not been able to do anything worth-while my whole life. How can I ever get out of this miserable rut? Tsk, tsk, tks, I say listen to yourself. Can you see how you are creating a self- fulfilling prophesy here? Sure if you continue to reject yourself and your abilities, others will reject you too, and so will your Human Spirit. That's the shocking truth. The Human Spirit will support, or give you back, whatever you put out to it. So, if you put out self-doubt, low self-esteem, and self- hatred, you will get more of it. That's what most people don't realize that the Human Spirit is essentially benevolent and it will give you whatever you seem to want. It doesn't judge what you send out into it, only responds or answer to it, "thinking" that that's what makes you happy. Weird, but true that is why it so crucial to send out only positive messages, because then the Human Spirit will sup- port them and give you more positive things in your life. That's called a process and a process never ends. Every single request you make of your Human Spirit is absolutely answered. I am not trying to scare you, but I am attempting to get you to accept responsibility for your actions. Manifesting using your mind, "as a man thinketh," is very powerful. There are consequences to every situation, some positive, some not. In any case, you must be ready to receive your answer and to love and work with the results. As the old adage goes, "Be careful what you ask for, because you just might get it!" In this process of manifesting you most surely will. You have heard people winning the lottery, a dream come true, and then losing it all. Money carries a certain obligation to use it wisely and manage it well. If the winner does not follow through on his part of the deal, he creates his own problems. Be ready for all aspects of your request to enter your life, and be willing to take the good with the bad. Accept that, you will surely build a positive, creative, abundant, and prosperous life, with a little help from the Holy Spirit within you. Remember *"For as he thinketh in his heart, so is he:" (Proverbs 23:7).*

I.

TAPPING INTO YOUR SPIRITUAL POWER

Getting your heart's desire requires you to send your message out to the Universe on more than one channel (using spiritual laws). That means you have to pack a lot of power in your punch! First you have to find that power, then direct and focus it on your intention or essence of what you want to materialize. The best and most effective way to do that is to use words and pictures. We must always create a mental image of what we want. In order to accomplish our goals we need the help of the tremendous power that lies within us. It is sometimes called our will, inner strength, higher self or Human Spirit. It will support us once we recognize and acknowledge it and demonstrate that we are up to the task ahead. It is really quite simple. We have to believe and trust in our own ability to receive the things we want in this life time. We must work with God's Spiritual Laws and understand how they operate.

They are:

1. SPIRIT CONTROLS MATTER

2. LESSER AUTHORITY YIELDS TO GREATER AUTHORITY

3. THE MIND IS THE ULTIMATE CONDUIT
    BETWEEN SPIRIT AND MATTER

4. SPEECH IS THE INTERMEDIATE CONDUIT
    BETWEEN SPIRIT AND MATTER AND BETWEEN
    GREATER AND LESSER AUTHORITY

I can almost hear that voice inside you say "Yeah, yeah, yeah, but will it really work?" I am here to tell you it does. Trust is the most important element in this whole process. Eliminate the negative thoughts that say, "It cannot be done." Each time you give in to a negative thought, you zap your power. Each time you buy into someone else's negativity, you take a step backward in your spiritual growth. For instance, when you allow another person to stop you from pursuing your dreams of a career, or the relocation of your home, or a long-desired adventure you'd like to try, you allow their fears, their reservations, or sometimes their jealousy to become more important than your needs. When you trust that you have what it takes to get what you want, and that there is some kind of spiritual order to the Universe, then you can truly begin to draw on your own personal power. If you believe that everything happens in life for a reason, it gets easier to accept your abilities. If you do your prep work and eliminate people or situations from your life that are negative and drain you of your enthusiasm, you will get rid of the doubt and truly see that all things are possible. Having said all that, you will need to zero in on what you truly want. To become real, our

21

desires must form deep within the core of our being. We must acknowledge what lies beneath the surface, in the heart of our request. Jesus said in Mark 11:24, *"Therefore I say unto you, What things soever ye desire, when ye pray, believe that ye receive them, and ye shall have them."*

II.

UNDERSTANDING THE ESSENCE OF YOUR INTENTION

Whatever you want, it will only come to you if you truly want it with every fiber of your being. It is not enough to give lip service to an idea. You have really got to want it in your heart and soul. Lots of times we feel we want some- thing and later on, after thinking about it, we realize we did not want it at all. I am convinced that is where the line, "Be careful what you wish for, you just might get it," came from. It is all about knowing – knowing, without a doubt, the very essence of what you want. It is only then that you can get it. The essence or basis of what you want is what I am talking about. For instance, if you think you want lots of money in your life, think again. Are your bills always greater than your income? Can you never make ends meet? Do you have a good job but there is never enough money in your bank account to cover all you expenses with some left for fun? These troubles could describe a per- son who is fortunate in that he or she has a good job but is creating struggle and scarcity in life. It is not really a lot of money this person needs, but financial security. For instance, let us assume you feel that if you had a certain sum of money your struggles would be over and your finances would stabilize.   Let   us say that the amount was $10,000.00. You then ask for and receive it from God, but when that is gone you are right back where you started. Rather, it is better to ask for an end to struggle and scarcity – then you will not need the $10,000.00 at all because you will have removed the problem. The essence of this intention is financial security, prosperity, and abundance. Ask for something greater than just a sum of money and you will be creating lifelong happiness. Try creating all the wealth you will ever need, instead of getting a limited amount. That way you will always have enough for everything you want. Think about that.

III.

WHERE DO WE BEGIN?

All pro-creation begins in the mind. Thought produces physical reality. Courage and tenacity get results. Pictures begin in the mind. Form pictures of yourself in your mind as though you have already achieved what you desire (Mark 11:24). See yourself successful, thin, rich, or happy. Your original idea is the nucleus for growth and manifestation in your life. When it is completed, thought becomes more than what it was. It becomes reality. Knowing what you want, identifying the essence of your intention will create successful results. Confusion creates mediocre or nonexistent results. That is why you sometimes get what you want, and sometimes you do not. You might not have understood your intention. Spend time thinking about what you want. It must be definite and heartfelt. Just keep reminding yourself that "you are a spirit, you have a soul and you live in your body." Remember that poverty is a mental illness. There is no virtue in poverty. It is an illness like any other mental illness. If you were physical ill, you would realize there was something wrong with you. You would seek help and try to get a cure for the condition at once. In the same way, if you do not have enough money constantly circulating in your life, there is something radically wrong with you. The urge of the life principle in you is to- ward growth, expansion, and the life more abundant. Jesus did not leave here for us to live in shacks, dress in rags, and go hungry. You should be happy, prosperous, and successful. Jesus said, *"...I am come that they may have life and have it more abundantly..." (John 10:10).*

IV.

THE MARVELOUS POWER OF YOUR SPIRIT

Once you learn to contact and release the hidden power of your spirit, you can bring into your life more power, more wealth, more health, more happiness and more joy. You do not need to acquire this power, because you already possess it. *"And God said, Let us make man in our image, after our likeness: and let them have dominion over the fish of the sea, and over the foul of the air, and over the cattle, and over all the earth..." Gen. 1:26.* We have this power because God gave it to mankind. You already have all of the power you will ever need. You will need to learn how to use it. You must understand the source of your power so that you can apply it in all departments of your life. If you follow the simple techniques and processes explained in this book, you can gain the necessary knowledge and understanding. You can be inspired by a new light, and generate a new force that enables you to realize your hopes and make all your dreams come true. Decide now to make your life grander, greater, richer, and nobler than ever before. Within your spirit depths lay infinite wisdom, infinite power, and an infinite supply of all that is necessary. It is waiting there for you to give it development and expression. Whatever you feel as true subjectively is expressed as conditions, experiences, and events. Motion and emotion must balance. This is the great law of life. You will find throughout all nature the laws of action and reaction (Law of Reciprocity) of rest and motion. These two must balance, so there will be harmony and equilibrium. You are here to let the life principle flow through you rhythmically and harmoniously. The intake and the outgo must equal also, the impression and the expression.

The 10 SPIRITUAL DNA Strands

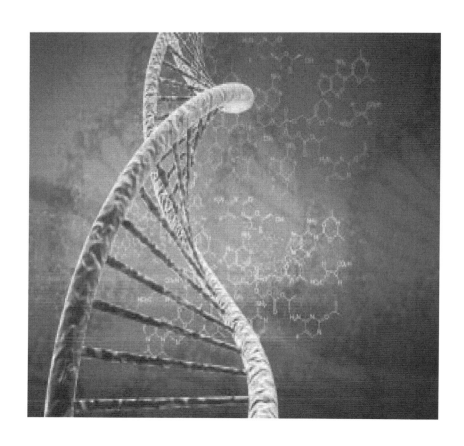

CHAPTER THREE

THE LAW OF THE SPIRIT AND SOUL

Objective and Subjective Mind

To live a victorious life 365 day a year and to have all of the blessings of God come into your life, you must understand how your mind works. You have two minds: conscious and subconscious. Your conscious mind (soul) is some- times referred to as your objective mind because it deals with outward objects. The objective mind is aware of the objective world. Its media of observation are your five physical senses. Your objective mind is your guide and director in your con- tact with your environment. You gain knowledge through your five senses. Your objective mind learns through observation, experience, and education. The greatest function of the objective mind is that of reasoning. Suppose you are one of the hundreds of thousands of tourists who visit the Grand Canyon every year. You would come to the conclusion that it is one of the world's most amazing natural wonders. This conclusion would be based on your observation of its incredible depth, the complex shaping of the rock formations, the beautiful play of colors among the different geological strata. This is the working of your objective mind. Your subconscious mind (Human Spirit) is often referred to as your subjective mind. Your subjective mind is aware of its environment, but not by means of the physical senses. Your subjective mind perceives by intuition. It is the seat of your emotions and the storehouse of memory. Your subjective mind performs its highest functions when your objective senses are not functioning. In other words, it is that intelligence that makes itself known when the objective mind is suspended or in a sleepy, drowsy state. Your subjective mind (Human Spirit) sees without the use of the natural organs of vision. It has the capacity of clairvoyance and clairaudience: it can see and hear events that are taking place elsewhere. Our spirit can leave our body (astral projection), travel to distant lands, and bring back information that is often of the most exact and truthful character. This is why Satan wants to possess your spirit. Through your subjective mind (Human Spirit) you can read thoughts of others, read the contents of sealed envelopes, or intuit the information on a computer disk without using a disk drive. Once we understand the interaction of the objective (soul) and subjective (spirit) minds, we are in a better position to learn the true art of prayer.

I.

THE HUMAN SPIRIT CANNOT REASON LIKE YOUR CONSCIOUS MIND

Your subconscious mind (Human Spirit) does not have the ability to argue or dispute what it is told. If you give it wrong information, it will accept it as true. It will then work to make that information correct. It will bring your suggestions, even those that were false, to pass as conditions, experiences, and events. Everything that has happened to you happened because of thoughts impressed on your Human Spirit through belief. If you have communicated wrong or distorted concepts to your Human Spirit, it is of the most urgent importance to correct them. The sure way to do this is by repeatedly giving your Human Spirit constructive, harmonious thoughts. As these are frequently repeated, your Human Spirit constructive, harmonious thoughts. As these are frequently repeated, your Human Spirit accepts them. In this way, you can form new, healthier habits of thought and life, for your Human Spirit is the seat of habit. The habitual thinking of your conscious mind establishes deep grooves in your Human Spirit. If habitual thoughts are harmonious, peaceful, and constructive, your Human Spirit will respond by creating harmony, peace, and constructive conditions. Have you become prey to fear, worry, and other destructive forms of thinking? The remedy is to recognize the power of your Human Spirit and decree freedom, happiness, and perfect health. Your Human Spirit being creative and one with the Holy Spirit will then start to create the freedom and happiness you have earnestly decreed.

II.

THE TREMENDOUS POWER OF SUGGESTION
(Positive and Negative Confession)

As you can see by what we have already discussed, your conscious mind serves as the "watchman at the gate." One of its most crucial functions is to protect your subconscious mind from false impressions. The reason this is so important goes back to one of the basic laws of mind: Your Human Spirit is very sensitive to suggestion. As you know, your subconscious mind does not make comparison or contrasts. It doesn't reason and think things out for itself. This latter function belongs to your conscious mind. No, your Human Spirit reacts to the impression given to it by your conscious mind. It does not pick and choose among different courses of action. It merely takes what it is given. Suggestion is a tremendously powerful force. Imagine that you are on board a ship that is rocking a bit from side to side. You approach a timid-looking fellow passenger and say, "Gee, you don't look so hot. Your face is practically green! I'm afraid you are about to be seasick. Can I help you to your cabin?" The passenger turns pale. The suggestion you have just made about seasickness links up with her fears and forebodings. She lets you escort her down below decks. Once she is there, the negative suggestion, which she accepted comes true.

III.

DIFFERENT REACTIONS TO THE SAME SUGGESTION

It is important to realize that different people will react in different ways to the same suggestion. This is because they have different subconscious conditioning or beliefs. Suppose, instead of choosing a fellow passenger on the ship, you go up to a member of the crew. You say, "Hey, buddy, you don't look so great. Do you think you are about to be seasick?" Depending on the sailor's temperament, he either laughs at your feeble joke or tells you to get lost. Your suggestion had no power over him, because the idea of seasickness was associated in is mind with his own immunity from it. Therefore, it called up not fear or worry, but self-confidence. A dictionary will tell you that a suggestion is the act or instance of putting something into one's mind. It is the mental process by which the thought or idea that has been suggested is entertained, accepted, or put into effect. Remember, a suggestion cannot impose itself on the Human Spirit against the will of the conscious mind. Your conscious mind has the power to reject the suggestion. The sailor had no fear of seasickness. He had convinced himself of his immunity, so the negative suggestion had no power to evoke fear. But your fellow passenger was already worried about becoming sick. Therefore your suggestion had power over her. All of us have our own inner fears, beliefs, and opinions. These inner assumptions rule and govern our lives. A suggestion has no power in and of itself. Its power arises from the fact that you accept it mentally. Only at that point do your Human Spirit powers begin to act according to the nature of the suggestion. You must be very careful to give your sub- conscious only those suggestions that heal, bless, elevate, and inspire you in all your ways. Remember, your Human Spirit does not understand a joke. It takes you at your word.

IV.

HOW AUTOSUGGESTION BANISHES FEAR

The term autosuggestion means suggesting something definite and specific to oneself. Like any tool, wrongly used it can cause harm, but used properly it can be extremely helpful.

V.

HAVE YOU ACCEPTED ANY OF THESE?

From the day we are born, we are bombarded with negative suggestions. Not knowing how to counter them, we unconsciously accept them and bring them into being as our experience. According to II Corinthians 10:3-5 negative suggestions become strongholds, *"For though we walk in the flesh, we do not war after the flesh: (For the weapons of our warfare are not carnal, but mighty through God to the pulling down of strongholds ;) Casting down imaginations, and every high thing that exalteth itself against the knowledge of God, and bringing into captivity every thought to the obedience of Christ."*

Here are some examples of negative suggestions:

- **You cannot.**
- **You will never amount to anything.**
- **You must not.**
- **You will fail.**
- **You have not got a chance.**

- **You are all wrong.**

- **It is no use.**

- **It is not what you know, but who you know.**

- **The world is going to the dogs.**

- **What is the use, nobody cares.**

- **There is no point to trying so hard.**

- **You are too old now.**

- **Things are getting worse and worse.**

- **Life is an endless grind.**

- **Love is for the birds.**

- **You just cannot win.**

- **Watch out, you will catch a terrible disease.**

- **You cannot trust a soul.**

By accepting hetero-suggestions of this kind, you collaborate in bringing them to pass. As a child, you were helpless when faced with the suggestions of others who were helpless when faced with the suggestions of others who were important to you. You did not know any better. The mind both conscious and unconscious was a mystery you did not even wonder about. As an adult, however, you are able to make choices. You can use constructive auto suggestions, which is a reconditioning therapy, to change the impressions made on you in the past. The first step is to make yourself aware of the hetero- suggestions that are operating on you. Unexamined, they can create behavior patterns that cause failure in your personal and social life. Constructive autosuggestion can release you from the mass of negative verbal conditioning that might other- wise distort your life pattern, making the development of good habits difficult or even impossible.

VI.

YOU CAN COUNTERACT NEGATIVE SUGGESTIONS

Pick up the paper or turn on the television news. Every day, you hear dozens of stories that could sow the seeds of futility, fear, worry, anxiety, and impending doom. If you accept them and take them in, these thoughts of fear can cause you to lose the will for life. However, once you under- stand that you do not have to accept them, choices open up for you. You have within you the power to counteract all these destructive ideas by giving your Human Spirit constructive autosuggestions. In themselves, the suggestions of others have no power over you. Whatever power they have, they gain because you give it to them through your own thoughts. You have to give your mental consent. You have to entertain and accept the thought. At that point it becomes your own thought, and your Human Spirit works to bring it into experience.   Remember, you have the capacity to choose. Choose life! Choose love! Choose health!

VII.

THE POWER OF AN ASSUMED MAJOR PREMISE

Since the days of ancient Greece, philosophers and logicians have studied the form of reasoning called a syllogism. Your mind reasons in syllogisms. In practical terms, this means that whatever major premises your conscious mind assumes to be true, that determines the conclusion your Human Spirit will come to, no matter what the particular question or problem might be. If your premises are true, the conclusion must be true.

For example:

• Every virtue is praiseworthy;

• Kindness is a virtue;

Therefore, kindness is praiseworthy.

Or this:

• All formed things change and pass away;

• The Pyramids of Egypt are formed things;

Therefore, the Pyramids will change and pass away. The first statement is referred to as the major premise, and the right conclusion must necessarily follow the right premise.

VIII.

THE HUMAN SPIRIT DOES NOT ARGUE CONTROVERSIALLY

Your Human Spirit is still all-wise. It knows the answers to all questions. However, it does not know that it knows. It does not argue with you or talk back to you. It does not say, "You must not impress me with suggestions of that sort." When you say, "I cannot do this," "I was born on the wrong side of the tracks," "I do not know the right politician," you are impregnating your subconscious with these negative thoughts. It responds accordingly. You are actually blocking your own good. You are bringing lack, limitation, and frustration into your life. When you set up obstacles, impediments, and delays in your conscious mind, you are denying the wisdom and intelligence resident in your subconscious mind. You are actually saying in effect that your subconscious mind cannot solve your problem. This leads to mental and emotional congestion, followed by sickness and neurotic tendencies. To realize your desires and overcome your frustration, affirm boldly several times a day. I HAVE A RIGHT TO BE HEALTHY, RICH, AND HAPPY ACCORDING TO II CORINTHIANS 8:9. The Holy Spirit that gave me this desire leads, guides, and reveals to me the perfect plan for the unfolding of my desire. I know the deeper wisdom of my spirit now responding, and what I feel and claim within is expressed in the without. There is a balance equilibrium, and equanimity. On the other hand, if you say, "There is no way out: I am lost; there is no way out of this dilemma; I am stymied and blocked," you will get no answer or response from your Human Spirit. If you want the Human Spirit and the Holy Spirit to work for you, you have to give it the right request and get its cooperation. It is always working for you. It is controlling your heartbeat and breathing this minute. When you cut your finger, it sets in motion the complex process of healing. Its most fundamental tendency is life-ward. It is forever seeking to take care of you and preserve you. Your Human Spirit has a mind of its own, but it accepts your patterns of thought and imagery. When you look for the answer to a problem, your Human Spirit will respond, but it expects you to come to a decision and to a true judgment in your conscious mind. You must acknowledge that the answer is in your Human Spirit. If you say, "I don't think there is any way out; I am all mixed up and confused; why don't I get an answer?" You are neutralizing your prayer. Like the solider marking time, you use up vital energy but you do not move forward. Still the wheels of your mind – relax, let go, and quietly affirm. My spirit knows the answer. It is responding now. I give thanks be- cause I know the Holy Spirit and my spirit knows all things and is revealing the perfect answer to me now. My real conviction is now set- ting me free the majesty and glory of my Human Spirit. I rejoice that it is so.

IX.   .

THE MIRACLE-WORKING POWER OF YOUR HUMAN SPIRIT

The power of your Human Spirit is beyond all measures. It inspires you and guides you. It calls up vivid scenes from the storehouse of memory. Your Human Spirit controls your heartbeat and the circulation of your blood. It regulates your digestion, assimilation, and elimination. When you eat a piece of bread, your Human Spirit transmutes it into tissue, muscle, bone, and blood. These processes are beyond the common intelligence of the wisest person who walks the earth. Your Human Spirit controls all the vital processes and functions of your body. It knows the answer to all problems. Your Human Spirit never sleeps or rests. It is always on the job. You can discover the miracle-working power of your spirit by plainly stating to your spirit prior to sleep that you want a specific thing accomplished. You will be amazed and delighted to discover that forces within you will be released that lead to the result you wished for. Here is a source of power and wisdom that puts you directly in touch with omnipotence (Holy Spirit). This is the power that moves the world, guides the planets in their course, and causes the sun to shine. Your Human Spirit is the source of your ideals, aspirations, and altruistic urges. It was through the Human Spirit that Shakespeare perceived and communicated great truths hidden from the average man of his day. It was through the Human Spirit that the Greek sculptor, Phidias, gained the art and skill to portray beauty, order, symmetry, and proportion in marble and bronze. The Human Spirit is the deep well from which great artists draw their awe-provoking power. It enabled the great Italian artist, Raphael, to paint his Madonna, and the great German musician, Beethoven, to compose his symphonies. Your Human Spirit can give you independence of time and space. It can make you free of all pain and suffering. It can give you the answer to all problems, whatever they may be. There is a power and an intelligence within you that far transcends your intellect, causing you to marvel at the wonder of it all. All these experiences cause you to rejoice and believe in the miracle-working powers of your own Human Spirit.

X.

YOUR HUMAN SPIRIT IS YOUR BOOK OF LIFE

Whatever thoughts, beliefs, opinions, theories, or dogmas you write, engrave, or impress on your Human Spirit, you will experience them as the objective manifestation of circumstances, conditions, and events. What you write on the inside, you will experience on the outside. You have two sides to your life, objective and subjective, visible and invisible, thought and its manifestation. Your thought is received as a pattern of neutral firings in your cerebral cortex, which is the organ of your conscious reasoning mind. Once the conscious (soul) or objective mind accepts the thought completely, it is transmitted to the other parts of the brain, where it becomes flesh and is made manifest in your experience. As previously outlined, your Human Spirit cannot argue. It acts only from what you write on it. It accepts your verdict or the conclusions of your Human Spirit as final. This is why you are always writing on the "book of life," because your thoughts become your experiences. The

American philosopher, Ralph Waldo Emerson, said, "Man is what he thinks all day long."

XI.

WHAT IS IMPRESSED IN THE HUMAN SPIRIT IS EXPRESSED

William James, the father of American psychology, said that the power to move the world is in your Human Spirit. Your Human Spirit is one with infinite (God) intelligence and boundless wisdom. It is fed by hidden springs and is called the "Law of Life." Whatever you impress upon your Human Spirit, the latter will move heaven and earth to bring it to pass. You must, therefore, impress it with right ideas and constructive thoughts. The reason there is so much chaos and misery in the world is that so many people do not understand the interaction of their conscious (soul) and subconscious (spirit) minds. When these two principles are in accord, in concord, in peace, and synchronously together, you will have health, happiness, peace, and joy. There is no sickness or dis- cord when the conscious and subconscious work together peacefully. In other words, whatever you impress in your Human Spirit that becomes expressed on the screen of space. The same truths were proclaimed by Moses, Isaiah, Jesus, Buddha, Zoroaster, Laotze, and all the illumined seers of the ages. Whatever you feel as true subjectively is expressed as conditions, experiences, and events.

Motion and emotion must balance. As in heaven (your own mind), so on earth (in your body and environment). This is the great Law of Life. You will find throughout all nature the law of action and reaction, of rest and motion. These two must balance then there will be harmony and equilibrium. You are here to let the life principle flow through you rhythmically and harmoniously. The intake and the outgo must be equal. The impression and the expression must be equal. All your frustration is due to unfulfilled desire. If you think negatively, destructively, and viciously, these thoughts generate destructive emotions that must be expressed and must find and outlet. These emotions, being of a negative nature, are frequently expressed as ulcers, heart trouble, tension and anxieties. What is your idea or feeling about yourself now? Every part of your being expresses that idea. Your vitality, body, financial conditions, friends, and social status represent a perfect reflection of the idea you have of yourself. This is the real meaning of what is impressed in your Human Spirit and what is expressed in all phases of your life.

XII.

HOW THE HUMAN SPIRIT CONTROLS ALL FUNCTIONS OF THE BODY

Whether you are awake or asleep, the ceaseless, tireless action of your subconscious mind controls all the vital functions of your body without any need for your conscious mind to intervene.

While you are asleep, your heart continues to beat rhythmically. Your chest and diaphragm muscles pump air in and out of your lungs. There the carbon dioxide that is the byproduct of the activity of your body's cells is exchanged for fresh oxygen you need to go on functioning. Your spirit controls your digestive processes and glandular secretions, as well as all the other wondrously complex operations of your body. All this happens whether you are awake or asleep. If you were forced to operate your body's functions with your conscious mind, you would certainly fail. You would probably die a very quick death. The processes are too complicated, too intertwined. The "heart-lung" machine that is used during open-heart surgery is one of the wonders of modern medical technology, but what it does is infinitely simpler than what your spirit does twenty-four hours a day, year out. Suppose you were crossing the ocean in a supersonic jetliner and you wandered into the cockpit. You certainly would not know how to fly the plane, but you would not find it difficult to distract the pilot and cause a problem. In the same way, your conscious mind cannot operate your body, but it can get in the way of proper operation. Worry, anxiety, fear, and depression interfere with the normal functioning of the heart, lungs, stomach, and intestines. The medical community is just beginning to appreciate how serious so-called "stress-related" diseases are. The tension is that these patterns of thought interfere with the harmonious functioning of your Human Spirit. When you feel physically and mentally disturbed, the best thing you can do is let go, relax, and still the wheels of your thought processes. Speak to your spirit. Tell it to take over in peace, harmony, and divine order. You will find that all the functions of your body will become normal again. Be sure to speak to your spirit with authority and conviction. It will respond by carrying out your command.

XIII.

HOW TO GET YOUR HUMAN SPIRIT TO WORK FOR YOU

The first thing to realize is that your spirit is always working. It is active night and day, whether you act upon it or not. Your Human Spirit is the builder of your body, but you cannot consciously perceive or hear that inner silent process. Your business is with your conscious mind (soul) and not your subconscious mind (spirit). Just keep your conscious mind (soul) busy with the expectation of the best, and make sure the thoughts you habitually think are based on things that are lovely, true, just, and harmonious. Begin now to take care of your conscious mind (soul), knowing in your heart and soul that your subconscious mind (spirit) is always expressing, reproducing, and manifesting according to your habitual thinking. Remember, just as water takes the shape of the pipe it flows through, the life principle in you flows through you according to the nature of your thoughts. Claim that the healing presence in your spirit is flowing through you as harmony, health, peace, joy, and abundance. Think of it as a living intelligence, a lovely companion on the way. Firmly believe it is continually flowing through you vivifying, inspiring, and prospering you. It will respond exactly this way. It is done unto you as you believe.

XIV.

HEALING PRINCIPLE OF THE HUMAN SPIRIT (SUBCONSCIOUS MIND) RESTORES OPTIC NERVES

One of the most celebrated healing shrines in the world is at Lourdes, in southwestern France. The archives of the medical department of Lourdes are with dossiers that detail well-authenticated cases of what are termed miraculous healings. One example among many is the case of Madame Bire, who was blind, with optic nerves that were atrophied and useless. After she visited Lourdes, she regained her sight. Several doctors who examined her testified that her optic nerves were still useless, and yet, she saw! A month later, a re-examination found that her visual mechanism had been fully restored to normal. I am thoroughly convinced that Madame Bire was not healed by the waters of the shrine. What healed her was her own subconscious mind, which responded to her belief. The healing principle within her subconscious mind responded to the nature of her thought. Belief is a thought in the Human Spirit. It means to accept something as true. The thought accepted executes itself automatically. Undoubtedly, Madame Bire went to the shrine with expectancy and great faith. She knew in her heart she would receive a healing. Her spirit responded accordingly, releasing the ever present healing forces.

TRICHOTOMY

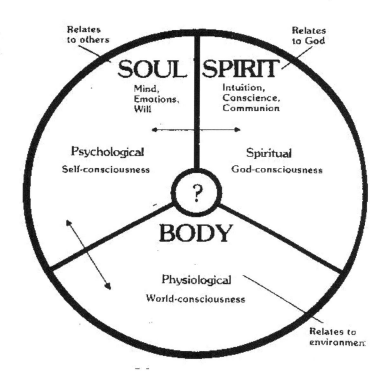

"…I pray God your whole spirit and soul and body be preserved blameless unto the coming of our Lord Jesus Christ."   I Thess.5:23

BRAIN WAVE FREQUENCY

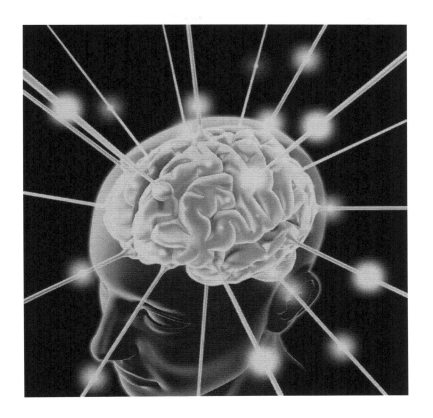

MEDITATION

This book of the law shall not depart out of thy mouth; but thou shalt meditate therein day and night, that thou mayest observe to do according to all that is written therein: for then thou shalt make thy way prosperous, and then thou shalt have good success.   Joshua 1:8

CHAPTER FOUR

HOW TO DEVELOP THE HUMAN SPIRIT

Science has spent millions of dollars to develop the physical body of man. Additional millions have been spent developing man's intellectual processes, which are a part of man's soul. But we know so little and have done so little about developing the spirit of man. Man's spirit can be educated, however; it can be educated and improved just as his mind can be educated and improved. The spirit can be trained and built up in strength just as the body can be built up in strength just as the body can be built up. How? THROUGH THE STUDY OF GOD'S WORD. We cannot understand spiritual things with our natural minds (conscious). Our minds, (conscious and subconscious) have to be changed, renewed by God's power in order for us to fully understand the Word of God. The apostle Paul said, *"But the natural man receiveth not (does not understand) the things of the Spirit of God: for they are foolishness unto him; neither can he know them, because they are spiritually discerned (understood)" (I Cor. 2:14).* The Word of God is of the Spirit of God, for *"holy men of God spake as they moved by the Holy Ghost" (II Peter 1:21).* This is why the natural mind cannot understand God's Word—the Bible cannot be understood with the head. It can only be understood with the heart. We have to get the revelation of it in our spirit. When a man is born again and becomes a child of God, he can them understand the Bible and can learn of spiritual things. Paul said, he is a new creature in Christ Jesus. *"Therefore if any man be in Christ, he is a new creature: old things are passed away; behold all things are become new" (II Cor. 5:17).* This process of training the spirit, of building it up in spiritual things, is a daily thing. *"......Though our outward man perish, yet the in- ward man is renewed day by day" (II Cor. 4:16).* In Chapter two page eighteen, we established the fact that the "inward man" (Human Spirit) is the real man, the real you. When the body dies, the inward man still lives because Paul writing to the Philippians, said, *"For to me to live in Christ, and to die is gain" (Phil. 1:21).* This does away with the theory that when a man is dead that is the end of him, that he is dead just as a dog is dead. There certainly wouldn't be any gain to dying if man perished and that was the end of everything. This also does away with the theory of soul sleep, that when a person dies he just floats around like a cloud in the sky, for there would be no gain in that. It also does away with the theory of rein- carnation which teaches that after death a person can be born again into the world as a cow or a fly, or perhaps a horse or a cat. This could not be true for there would be no gain in coming back as some lower form of animal life. We need to stay with God's Word and not get off into foolish theories. Why did Paul say to die is to gain? It is surely no gain to us who lose our loved ones, but it is gain to them. Paul went on to say, *"For I am in a strait betwixt two, having a desire to depart, and to be with Christ; which is far better: Nevertheless to abide in the flesh is more needful for you"* (Phil. 1:23-24). The reason Paul said it was gain to die was that he would depart to be with Christ. Some people think that eternal life is only the life they are going to have when they get to heaven. However, it is something we have right now. Eternal life is the life of God. It is the God kind of life. Eternal life is the nature of God which comes into our spirit to re-create us and make us a new creature, to change our nature. Then we have within us the nature of God which is love. We have within us the love of God. *"By this shall men know that ye are my disciples, if ye have love one to another"* (John 13:35). When we have been born again and have this God nature abiding within us, we can develop our spirit to higher levels of worship and service of God. But before going further on this let us pause to review what we learned in chapter two on the subject of the three-fold nature of man—spirit, soul, and body. First of all, it is necessary that we differentiate between the three. Paul made a distinction between them. *"....I pray God your whole spirit and soul and body be preserved blameless unto the coming of our Lord Jesus Christ"* (I Thess. 5:23). Some have mistakenly thought that the spirit and soul is the same thing. However, the Bible says, *"For the word of God is quick, and powerful, and sharper than any two-edged sword, piercing even to the dividing asunder of soul and spirit..."* (Heb. 4:12). If the spirit and soul were one and the same, they could not be divided. As mentioned previously, man's three-fold nature is this: (1) Spirit (subconscious)—the part of man which deals with the spiritual realm; (2) Soul (conscious)—the part of man which deals with the mental realm, his reasoning and intellectual powers; (3) Body—the part of man which deals with the physical realm. Many find it difficult to differentiate be- tween the spirit (subconscious) and the soul (conscious). It is easier to differentiate between the body and the other two dimensions of man than it is to distinguish between the spirit and the soul. The only authority you can go to, to under- stand the difference between the two, is the Word of God, primarily the New Testament. The Old Testament was translated from the Hebrew and one word, sometimes translated as spirit, has been translated as twelve different things. Some of these are: wind, whirlwind, blast, mildew, breath, etc. I picked up a book once which was distributed by one of the false cults, and on the cover it said that when a man is dead, he is dead like a dog. As I read through the book I found their argument to be that the Old Testament speaks of the soul of animals, yet Christendom talks about a never-dying soul, that the soul will live forever. Both statements are correct, but require an explanation. It is true that in the original Hebrew the Bible does speak of the souls of animals. Animals do have souls because they have limited reasoning faculties, and these faculties are of the soul. Man's reasoning faculties are of his soul, and the animal's limited reasoning faculties of its soul. Animals also have affection, and this too is part of the soul. Now

51

when the Old Testament speaks about the spirit of an animal (as in Eccl. 3:21) it is talking about the breath of an animal. Animals are not spirits. They are merely soul and body. When animals die, that is the end. But man is not just soul and body as animals are. He is spirit, soul, and body. This book also claimed that the spirit of man and the breath of man were the same thing. If this were true, then when Paul said in Romans 1:9, *"For God is my witness, whom I serve with my spirit in the gospel of his Son…"* he was saying, *"I serve God with my breath."* Also, if "breath" and "spirit" was the same thing, then when Paul said, *"For if I pray in un- known tongue, my spirit prayeth . . ."* (*I Cor.14:14)*, he was saying, "When I pray with tongues, I pray with my breath." This doesn't make much sense, does it? Again, Paul said, *"But ye are come unto mount Sion, and unto the city of the living God… to God the Judge of all, and to the spirits of just men made perfect"* (*Heb. 12:22-23)*. If "spirit" means "breath," then Paul said, "We are come unto the breath of just men made perfect." This would mean that Jesus died to make our breath perfect. This sounds ridiculous, but if we assume that the two words mean the same thing, this is the logical pattern we would have to follow. Man, however, is a spirit. He has a three- fold nature. He is spirit, he possesses a soul, and he lives in a body. We sometimes hear the preacher say in church that souls came forward to be saved or that souls were born again. However, it is not the soul that is saved at that moment. It is not the soul that is born again. It is the spirit. The epistle of James was not written to sinners but to the church, for over and over again James says, *"Wherefore, my beloved brethren...lay apart all filthiness and superfluity of naughtiness, and receive with meekness the engrafted word, which is able to save your soul" (James 1:19-21).* Did James mean to say here, "which is able to save your spirit"? No, he meant just what he said. Let us look at the next verses to get the full import of what James is saying. *"But be ye doers of the word, and not hearers only, deceiving your own selves. For if any be hearer of the word, and not doer, he is like unto a man beholding his natural face in a glass: For he beholdeth himself, and goeth his way, and straightway forgetteth what manner of a man he was. But whoso looketh into the perfect law of liberty, and continueth therein, he being not a forgetful hearer, but a doer of the work, this man shall be blessed in his deed" (Verses 22-25)* James, who was talking to believers, was saying that if you want to get your soul (mind) saved now, and then you have to be a doer of the word and not just a hearer only. Paul, also writing to believers, wrote, *"I beseech you therefore, brethren, by the mercies of God, that ye present your bodies a living sacrifice, holy, acceptable unto God, which is your reasonable service. "And be not conformed to this world: but be ye transformed by the renewing of your mind, that ye may prove what is that good, and acceptable, and perfect, will of God" (Rom. 12:1-2).* Paul was saying the same thing that James was saying. Paul said to be "transformed by the renewing of your mind..." James said to "receive with meekness the engrafted word, which is able to save your souls." Both apostles were talking about renewing, restoring, saving, the mind, or the soul. The "engrafted word" which James referred to, will "save your soul," will renew your mind, will restore your soul. We see this also in the 23rd Psalm. "He restoreth my soul". This doesn't say that He restores my spirit. When something is restored we take what is already there and redo it. But our spirits are born of God. *"....That which is born of the Spirit is spirit" (John 3:6).* This Hebrew word translated "restore" means identically the same thing as the Greek word for "renew." Today we use the words "restore" and "renew" in the same way. For instance, an old piece of furniture can be renewed or restored. We save it, we don't let it go. It is saved by renewing it, by restoring it. This is what James was saying—as believers who have become new creatures in Christ Jesus, we are spiritually saved and have received eternal life. We should then receive the engrafted Word which will save, which will restore, which will renew our mind, our soul. This was something that the believers had to do for themselves. They were to renew their minds. They were to "save their souls." How? Through the Word of God! Why is it so essential that the mind be renewed? Even though your spirit is born again, even though your spirit has the Holy Spirit abiding within; if the mind isn't renewed (or as James said, the soul saved) with the Word, then the mind, which has been educated through the body and through the physical sensed, will side in with the body and the two will frame up on your spirit to keep you a baby Christian. Such immature Christians are carnal, or body-ruled (sense- ruled) Christians. Paul told the Corinthians, *"For ye are yet carnal..." (I Cor. 3:3).* One translation of this verse reads, "You are body-ruled." In other words, their bodies, through their un-renewed minds, were ruling their spirits, even though they were new creatures in Christ. They had never developed spiritually. Many Christians today will live and die as spiritual babies. The faith life will always be obscured to them. They will never understand faith. Yet we cannot fully live the Christian life unless we walk by faith, since the Bible says that we are to walk by faith and not by sight. Those who are living in the flesh are living in unbelief and are always engaged in warfare. Life is a battle for them. Their minds have never renewed with the Word of God and they don't know that Jesus has already won the battle. He has already whipped the foe. They don't know that the devil is a defeated foe. They are still trying to whip him. They are trying to fight the devil in their own power. And some have fought until they have fought themselves completely out of everything. They live and die without ever growing beyond the babyhood stage of Christianity. But when the mind has renewed with the Word of God, then the spirit through the renewed mind can control the body. The soul will then take sides with the spirit because it knows the Word. It is renewed with the Word. It will allow the spirit to dominate it. Then God's Spirit through man's spirit will dominate.

I.

BIBLICAL PRINCIPAL (NUMBER ONE):
MEDITATE IN THE WORD OF GOD

As we stated previously, it is possible to train and educate the Human Spirit just as it is possible to train and educate the human soul, or mind. Sermons which I have preached in my church and in revivals on the subject of man on three dimensions—spirit, soul, and body – I have used sermons with a four biblical principal formula to help believers in understanding their spiritual lives. Any formula we might use must, first of all, be based on God's Word. Jesus said, *"...Man shall not live by bread alone, but by every word that proceedeth out of the mouth of God" (Matt. 4:4).* God's Word is spirit food. It will build up our spirits. God is a Spirit. Man, who is made in the likeness and image of God, is also a spirit creature. He is in the same class of being as God. Man is a spirit. He possesses a soul and lives in a body. At the creation of man, God placed within man a yearning, a heart hungry for fellowship with Him. But then Adam sinned in the garden, he fell and his spirit became estranged from God. How- ever, because of this yearning and heart hunger for fellowship with his Creator, man's spirit, apart from God, is never satisfied. This is what drives him out into the world seeking pleasures and material things. He is trying to find satisfaction for the heart hunger inside him. This spirit hunger has driven many, in ignorance, to false cult and has given birth too many religions of the world. But it cannot be satisfied until we become acquainted with the Lord Jesus Christ and receive eternal life. It cannot be satisfied until we become a child of God and are back in fellowship with Him. The spirit is the part of man which contacts God. In the new birth the spirit is made a new creature. *"Therefore if any man be in Christ, he is a new creature..." (II Cor. 5:17).* This new man that we have become in Christ Jesus should dominate our thinking processes and should dominate our body. Yet many who are born again and who are even filled with the Holy Spirit are still baby Christians and have not developed spiritually. The Corinthian's were born again. They had received the Holy Spirit and the gifts of the Spirit were manifest among them. Yet Paul reproved them for being baby Christians. He said of them, *". . . Ye come behind in no gift. ." (I Cor. 1:7).* But still they were carnal. They were baby Christians. Some people think that because individual spiritual gifts operating in their lives they are fully grown mature Christians. However, baby Chris- tians can have the gifts as well as mature Chris- tians, as Paul states here. Spiritual gifts don't make one a fully developed Christian. We have to grow in God. The fact that these gifts are sometimes manifested through immature Christians doesn't mean that they are not genuine gifts. If God had to wait until we were perfect before he could use us, he could never use any of us. In fact, he could not have used the apostles either for they weren't perfect. Reading in the New Testament we see where some of them had their differences.

I have seen some of the most miraculous things come about out of the mouths of babes, so to speak. The ideal, of course, is for people to grow up and develop the fruits of the spirit as well as spiritual gifts. Baby Christians are the results of the fact that their salvation experience and their experience of being baptized in the Holy Ghost has not yet affected their bodies and their minds. As we mentioned earlier, the Bible tells us that we ourselves must do something with our minds. *"Present your bodies a living sacrifice, holy, acceptable unto God, which is your reasonable service. And be not conformed to this world: but be ye trans- formed by the renewing of your mind, that ye may prove what is that good, and acceptable, and perfect, will of God" (Rom 12:1-2).* When we are born of God and have the life of God in us, then the Holy Ghost comes in to fill us and to help us. He is our Helper. He will help us to present our bodies to God as a living sacrifice. The Word of God was given to us by the Holy Spirit to develop our spirit nature, the new man on the inside. If we want to educate and train our spirit, then number one in our biblical principle formula is: Meditate in the Word of God. This does not mean we are just to read the Word. We can say, "Oh, I read so many chapters," all we want, but it doesn't amount to anything unless we take time to mediate in God's Word. To make clear what we mean by "meditate in God's Word," let us look into the book of Joshua. When God appointed Joshua to be Moses' successor and lead the children of Israel, He said to Joshua, *"This book of the law shall not depart out of thy mouth; but thou shalt meditate therein day and night, that thou mayest observe to do according to all that is written therein: for then thou shalt make thy way prosperous, and then thou shalt have good success" (Josh. 1:8).* Do you want to be prosperous? God tells us how. He tells us here in His Word that if His Word fills our hearts to the extent that we" mediate therein day and night," and that we "observe to do according to all what is written therein," then we shall find prosperity. It goes without saying that a man who is filled with God's Word will prosper spiritually. But the point I want to emphasize here is God's promise of physical prosperity as well as spiritually prosperity. So many times we pray, "God prosper us." But just to pray this prayer without following God's formula won't work. God has a way of doing it and that way is through His Word. God promised success in this life, but most of us have made some mistakes. We have erred in business matters, perhaps lost money or spent be- yond our means. We didn't deal wisely in the affairs of this life. However, if we will follow God's plan, His instructions for a successful life, we needn't make these mistakes. We can "deal wisely in the affairs of life." We can become successful and prosperous. If we don't we have not one to blame but ourselves, for God has provided the way whereby we can succeed. God does it, but we have our part to play. Too many times we think we can ignore God's Word and can get the job done by praying. If we could just do enough praying, if we could just pray loudly enough and long enough, we reason, if we could just get enough people praying for us, it would work. But it won't! Prayer has its place, and I would certainly be the last to belittle the importance of prayer. But, if we are not going to do what God's Word says to do, we can pray forever that God will prosper us, we can persuade all the preachers and their wives that we know to pray for us, and when they all get through praying we will be no better off than we were before unless we are going to do what God's Word says to do. Jesus said, *"... The words that I speak unto you, they are spirit, and they are life" (John 6:63).* He also said, *"Heaven and earth shall pass away, but my words shall not pass away" (Matt. 24:35).* The Bible tells us that God has magnified His Word above his name (Psalm 138:2). So the first step in beginning the development of our spirit is to take time to meditate in the Word. Some tremendous thoughts in connection with the development of the spirit life are found in the New Testament. In this dispensation of grace we are at an advantage, for we have a better covenant with better promises. If believers living in Old Testament times could make their way prosperous and could have good success, what should we do with a better covenant, with better promises? We should have super-prosperity and super- success. Jesus said, *"And I will pray the Father, and he shall give you another Comforter (or Helper' as it reads in the Greek), that he may abide with you forever; Even the Spirit of truth; whom the world cannot receive, because it seeth him not, neither knoweth him: but ye know him; for he dwelleth with you, and shall be in you" (John 14:16-17).*

What is this Holy Spirit going to do when He dwells in you? *"Howbeit when he, the Spirit of truth, is come, he will guide you into all truth: for he shall not speak of himself; but whatsoever he shall hear, that shall he speak: and will show you things to come. He shall glorify me: for he shall receive of mine, and shall show it unto you" (John 16:13-14).* The spiritual development that we should have had as a result of the indwelling Holy Spirit has slipped by us. Why? If the devil can he will keep us from getting the truth. He will sidetrack us and get us into some other spiritual (demonic) realm. Most Spirit-filled people don't realize what they have and are not walking in the light of what they have. I have heard people testify that they are filled with the Holy Ghost, then five minutes later they are down at the alter praying, "Lord, give me power." If you have the Holy Ghost, you have the Powerhouse within you. The thing you need to do is to learn to cooperate with him, to know what He is going to do in you and learn to listen to Him. He is in there and He will guide you into all truth. We also need to realize that the Holy Spirit is a gentleman. He is not going to come in if we don't want Him to. He is not going to come in and take over. He can help only as we respond to Him. The Power of God is passive until faith is exercised. Many times before going out to minister I have said to myself, "Greater is he that is in me than he that is in the world." "The Greater One is in there." When I have some job to do for which I feel inadequate I remind myself that the Holy Spirit is within me. "Greater is he that is in me." He is greater than the devil that is in the world. He is greater than the hatred that is in the world. "The Greater One is in me." When I have said, "The Greater One is in me," I have noticed His power rising up in me and giving illumination to my conscious mind and direction to my Human Spirit. I was able to walk out a conqueror and walk right over the top of the devil and all his cohorts. I learned early that he is in there and that greater is He that is in me than he that is in the world. Let us take time to meditate in the Word, in the new covenant. It will help to develop our spirit nature.

II.

BIBLICAL PRINCIPAL (NUMBER TWO): PRACTICE THE WORD OF GOD

The second biblical principal in our four biblical principal formulas for developing our spirit nature is this: Practice the Word. In our previous points we mentioned the importance of meditating in God's Word. Equally important, once we have God's Word firmly abiding in our hearts and minds, is to put it to use. *"But be ye doers of the word, and not hearers only ..."* *(James 1:22).* Earlier we referred to the passage in the epistle of James which says, *". . . Receive with meekness the engrafted word, which is able to save your souls. But be ye doers of the word, and not hearers only . . .for if any be a hearer of the word, and not a doer, he is like unto a man be- holding his natural face in a glass: For he beholdeth himself, and goeth his way, and straight- way forgetteth what manner of man he was"* *(James*

1:21-24). Apostle James said that once we receive the Word, we should act on it. We should put it into practice. We can meditate on God's Word and come to know what it says, but until we put it into practice it will do us not good. When God told Joshua to mediate in the Word *"day and night" (Josh. 1:8)*, he also went on to say "that thou mayest observe to do ..." in other words, after reading and meditating on the Word, do it! A doer of the Word is one who practices the Word, one who puts the Word into practice. It is one thing to hear it, but it is still another thing to do it. We have too many hearers, but not enough practices. Too many times we hear the Word. We even nod our heads in agreement and say, "Amen, brother that is all truth." But we don't go out and do it. And it cannot affect our lives until we apply it in our lives. It cannot help us until we put it into practice. How does one "practice the Word?" What did James mean when he said to be doers of the Word? Did he mean to keep the Ten Commandments? No, that isn't what he was talking about. Actually, the Ten Commandments were for spiritually dead people, they are not for spiritually alive people. Then we are not supposed to keep the Ten Commandments? someone might ask. Under the new covenant we have a new commandment. Jesus said, *"A new commandment I give unto you, That he love one another; as I have loved you, that ye also love one another" (John 13:34)*. If we obey this commandment it takes the place of all the rest. Also, if we have the love of God in our hearts, we will not steal from our fellow man. We will not murder our brother if we love him. Love does not hate. Love gives, it does not steal. God so loved us that He gave His Son to die for us that we might live. Apostle James also said that the man who is a hearer of the Word and not a doer deceives himself. Another word for this is "deludes" him-self. There are a lot of self-deluded people. The devil didn't delude them. He didn't deceive them. They have deceived and deluded themselves. Apostle James said that if we hear the Word but don't do it or practice it, we are deluding our- selves. We are the ones who did it, not the devil, not someone else. When Apostle James said to be a doer of the Word, he was telling believers to practice this Word of God, to put it into action in their daily lives. We are to walk in the light of the New Testament.

THE SELF-DELUDED

Apostle James is saying that the person who thinks that knowledge is all that is necessary will fail. It is the doer of the Word, the man who practices it, lives it, walks in it, that builds it into his own life, whom God honors. There is a grave danger of deluding our own selves. We know the Word. We may be familiar with the original Greek or Hebrew. We may know the history of the Word, but that is all wasted energy if we do not live the Word and practice it. When you come to a hard place, and need money, you resolutely turn to the Lord, because you know that "My God shall supply every need of yours." You have taken your place. You act the part of a real believer. Instead of turning to the beggarly elements of the world, you turn to the Father. Or if a loved one is sick, instead of being frightened, you remember the Word: "Surely He hath borne our sicknesses and carried our diseases. And we have come to esteem Him as the One who was stricken, smitten of God and afflicted with those diseases." We know it now. We act on that Word. We do not fear; we are not disturbed, because we know that the Word says that with His stripes we are healed. Or if some calamity has come, some rumor, the adversary has stirred things to our detriment, we know that the Word tells us in Isaiah 54:17, *"No weapon that is formed against thee shall prosper, and every tongue that shall rise against thee in judgment, thou shalt condemn. This is the heritage of the servants of the Lord, and their righteousness is of me, saith the Lord."* You see, you can trust Him. You bank on Him. Your expectations are from Him. You do not turn to the beggarly help of Sense Knowledge. We know the Word, we live the Word, we act the Word, we trust implicitly in the Word, and we know that God and His throne are back of every word. That gives us a quiet, restful confidence. John 15:5, 7, *"I am the vine; ye are the branches: He that abideth in me and I in him, the same beareth much fruit..."* What kind of fruit is it? It is love fruit; it is faith fruit; and it is prayer fruit. It is the same kind that Jesus bore. It will be doing what Jesus did. *"If ye abide in me, and my words abide in you, ask whatsoever ye will, and it shall be done unto you."* The doer abides in Christ, and His words are living in him in the measure that he lives them, does them, and practices them. All his decisions are made by the Word. He is living in the realm of the living Christ. Notice this eighth verse: "Herein is my Father glorified, that ye bear much fruit; and so shall ye be my disciples." What kind of fruit is it? It is the fruit that comes from the Word. The hearer may show many blossoms of promise, but it is the doer that delivers the ripened fruit. The Word lives in him; he lives in the Word. He is the fruit-bearing branch – a real doer. Prayer is a reality. He is not talking off into space. He is in the Throne Room in the presence of the Father. Here the Name of Jesus is al- ways honored. He receives that for which he asks. Did you notice, "As you live in me and my words live in you"? That is the real doing of the Word, not just a doctrine, but God speaking and God living in His own Word in us.

THE REAL DOER

James 2:20 (Moffatt), *"Faith without deeds is barren."* It is mere empty words – lovely, beautiful– but they are never crystallized or made real. Weymouth says, "Without corresponding actions." Unless you are a doer of the Word, you are not a believer of the Word. You have nothing but a Mental Assent without action, a mere empty profession of religion of words. Jesus would call them a sand foundation, just a sand house made by idle hands on the seashore to be destroyed by the next incoming tide. What a danger is a religion of words if there is no corresponding action.

If one is not a doer of the Word, he is a foolish builder on the sand of the Senses. Then I read where Apostle James said, *"My brethren, count it all joy when ye fall into divers temptations; knowing this, that the trying of your faith worketh patience"* *(James 1:2-3)*. The Greek word which is translated here "temptations" means "tests" or "trials." Apostle James didn't sway to count it all joy when every- thing is going well, when we have money in our pocket, when our bills are all paid and our children are all well. He said to count it joy when we meet tests and trials along the way. Why? Because out of tribulation comes victory. Are you counting your trials as joy? You should. Try it and you'll find that it makes all the difference in the world. We can thank God for every test and trial. This is what James is talking about when he said to be a doer of the Word. And this is something that we have to do for ourselves. I cannot be a doer of the Word for you. I can only be a doer of the Word for me. We can assist one another temporarily with our faith and prayers, but I am so glad that God has some- thing better for us than just an occasional blessing. This is an entire way of life—the faith life. So we have seen that to develop our spirit life we begin by meditating in the Word, and then we practice the Word in our daily lives. This will develop the inward man, and then the inward man (Human Spirit) will dominate the outward man. Worries and circumstances from the outside world cannot dominate us when our mind is renewed with the Word of God.

III.

BIBLICAL PRINCIPAL (NUMBER THREE):
GIVE FIRST PLACE TO THE WORD OF GOD

The two biblical principles that we have given thus far for cultivating the spirit of man are centered on the Word. Jesus said, *". . . Man shall not live by bread alone, but by every word that proceedeth out of the mouth of God" (Matt. 4:4).* On another occasion He said, *"...The words that I speak unto you, they are spirit, and they are life" (John 6:63).* The Bible also tells us, *"For all flesh is as grass, and all the glory of man as the flower of grass. The grass withereth, and the flower thereof falleth away: But the word of the Lord endureth forever...." (I Peter 1:24-25).*The Bible says concerning Jesus that He is "THE SURETY OF A BETTER TESTAMENT" (Heb. 7:22). The New Testament is the better covenant. Jesus is the surety of this better covenant. What does this mean? That Jesus stands behind every word from Matthew through Revelation. He stands back of every word to make it good. Jeremiah 1:12 says, *"... I will hasten my word to perform it."* Another translation says, "I watch over my word to perform it." In other words, the Lord watches over His Word to do it, to make it good. If we don't act on God's Word, if we don't practice God's Word, then He doesn't have anything to make good in our lives. He doesn't have anything to watch over. He doesn't have anything to hasten to fulfill, if we are not acting on His Word, if we are not a doer of His Word. But if we will stand by God's Word, He will stand by us. Thus, our spiritual development hinges on the Word of God because the Word has been given to build our spirit nature. Principle three, then, in this four-point formula is: Given the Word first place in your life. First of all, as we have said, we must mediate in the Word. We wouldn't be able to practice the Word if we didn't first know it. We couldn't be a doer of the Word if we didn't know it. We cannot do something that we do not know, so this is the reason we must first meditate on the Word. The Word doesn't become real to us until we know what it says and act on it. Then we should put God's Word first in our lives. We can become so Word-conscious that no matter what comes up, no matter what we may face, the first thing we think of is, "What does God's Word say?" Too few Christians are like that, however. When emergencies arise, most think first from the natural standpoint because they haven't soaked in the Word of God. They haven't built God's Word into their spirit. Therefore, something else comes to their minds and they rush to do something other than what God's Word says. We can feed upon God's Word until it be- comes a part of our inward nature, until in any situation or emergency, the first thing we think of inside us is what God's Word says. It will rise up in us and give illumination to our minds and direction to our spirits. People

often try to get advice from some- one else instead of listening to what God has to say about it. If people, even preachers, cannot advise you from the Word of God, their advice is very poor. We can sometimes get in real trouble by following the well-intentioned advice of fellow Christians who are not carefully attuned to God's Word. I did one time and almost died. Are you facing some problem in your life? Then find out what God's Word has to say about it. Meditate on the Word. Then practice the Word. Put that promise into action. Put God's Word first— not circumstances, not the well- meaning advice of friends and love ones, not our own personal feelings or desires—put God's Word first! We can find direction in God's Word, and if we will listen to the Holy Spirit, He will take the Word of God and direct us. He will take the Word and open it up to us. We already have direction from God for so many of the affairs of life. We just need to act on it. Make it a habit to ask yourself with regard to every aspect of life, "What does God's Word have to say about this?" Become so Word- conscious that you automatically check every thought and deed against God's Word to make sure you are in His will. In His Word we find the answer for every avenue of life. One promise in the Word says, *". . . Greater is he that is in you, than he that is in the world? (I John 4:4).* No matter what you may face, he that is in you is greater than your problem. Believing this you can face life fearlessly. You can face life with the spirit of a conqueror no matter what the circumstances.

IV.

BIBLICAL PRINCIPAL (NUMBER FOUR):
OBEY THE VOICE OF YOUR SPIRIT

Point number four in the development of our spirits is this: Instantly obey the voice of your spirit. Remember, God speaks to our spirit, He doesn't speak to our head. He communicates with our spirit and not our reasoning faculties. *"The spirit of man is the candle of the Lord . . ." (Prov. 20:27).* God informs our spirit and our spirit will pass that information on to our mind. The spirit has a voice. We call it guidance, intuition, an inward voice or conscience. The conscience is the voice of the spirit. The con- science of an unsaved man is an unsafe guide because if he has had any "Christian" training he is often dominated by that. And if he hasn't, his conscience will permit him to do a lot of things that are wrong. If a man is born again, his spirit has become a new spirit with the life and nature of God in it. If his spirit then has the privilege of feeding and meditating on God's Word, if he practices God's Word, and if he puts God's Word first in his life, then his conscience, the voice of his spirit, will be a safe guide and will become the voice of Gods speaking to him. I believe that if we will walk in fellowship with God through His Word through prayer, if we train our spirit through the Word of God and learn to instantly obey the voice of our spirit, then after a while we can know the will of God even in the minor details of life. Jesus said, *"I will pray the Father, and he shall give you another Comforter, that he may abide with you forever; Even the Spirit of truth; whom the world cannot receive, because it seeth him not, neither knoweth him: but ye know him; for he dwelleth with you, and shall be in you" (John 14:16-17).* Then He said,

"Howbeit when he, the Spirit of truth is come, he will guide you into all truth . . ." (John 16:13). I do not believe that Jesus was referring only to the revelation that was to be given to the apostle Paul concerning God's great plan of redemption. I believe it also means that the Spirit of God will guide each one of us in the affairs of life. We should begin our day with the consciousness that we have a Guide in us. We are not left with- out guidance, without direction. Jesus said, "He will guide you into all truth . . . he will show you things to come." Jesus did not just mean that the Spirit of God would only show the apostles what we have in the book of Revelation and the epistles about prophecy concerning future events. Certainly that was a part of it, but I believe it also means that in our personal lives the Spirit of God will show us things to come. He will show us things so that we can be ready for them, so that we won't be caught unaware. Too, He will show us some things that we can change. God, through His Spirit, told Isaiah to say to Hezekiah, *"Set thine house in order; for thou shalt die, and not live" (II Kings 20:1).* The Spirit of God was showing him something that was to come in the future. Under the present circumstances, the way things were, Hezekiah was going to die. But then Isaiah left Hezekiah's bed-chamber, Hezekiah turned his face to the wall, he wept and cried, he prayed and repented before God. Before Isaiah got out of the courtyard, God told him to return to Hezekiah and say, *"Thus saith the Lord, the God of David thy father, I have heard thy prayer, I have seen thy tears: be- hold, I will heel thee . . . I will*

add unto thy days fifteen years . . ." (II Kings 20:5-6). So we see here that God will sometimes show us things that can be changed. He may show us things about ourselves. He may show us things about our loved ones that we can change. Then there are some things we cannot change. They are coming, but we can be prepared for them. Jesus, speaking to His disciples, said, *". . . It is expedient for you that I go away: for if I go not away, the Comforter will not come unto you..." (John 16:7).* But He promised, *"I will pray the Father, and he shall give you another Comforter, that he may abide with you forever; Even the Spirit of truth; whom the world cannot receive, because it seeth him not, neither knoweth him: but ye know him; for he dwelleth with you, and shall be in you. I will not leave you comfortless..." (John 14:16-18).* We do not need to feel like an orphan in this world. There is no need to be desolate or isolated. We can know the strength of God in our spirit. We can have the power of God in our life. We can rise up like a strong man and do the works of God. Put the enemy to flight and the powers of darkness will flee before you. The devil will run from you. When he sees you coming, he will go the other direction because you are God's man, God's superman, God's man of power. Get thrilled with the Word of God and walk in the light of the Word. Claim that which the Word has promised and you will reap its benefits. When you become a doer of the Word and not a hearer only, you will become a recipient of the provisions He has made for you.

"Therefore I say unto you, What things soever ye desire, when ye pray, believe that ye receive them, and ye shall have them."

Mark 11:24

KEY SCRIPTURE READING

"But thou shalt remember the Lord thy God: For it is he that giveth thee power to set wealth, that he may establish his covenant which he sware unto thy Fathers..." Deut. 8:18

"... I am come that they might have life, and that they might have it more abundantly." John 10:10

"For whatsoever is born of God overcometh the world..." I John 5:4

CHAPTER FIVE

POSITIVE CONFESSION

"Death and life are in the power of the tongue." (Proverbs 18:21)

Our trained Human Spirit will only maintain a positive attitude if we continue training it with daily positive confessions. Christianity is confession from beginning to end. The Christian faith is not merely something we believe—it also involves what we say or confess, *"For with the heart man believeth unto righteousness; and with the mouth confession is made unto salvation" (Rom. 10:10).* The importance and necessity of confession is evident here, for as Jesus informs us in Matthew 10:32-33 and John 12:42-43, salvation involves confession as well as belief. We are admonished twice in the Book of Hebrews to *"Let us hold fast the profession of our faith without wavering" (Heb.10:23)*, and Jesus teaches us in Mark 11:23 that we can receive whatsoever we confess shall come to pass. Since *"death and life are in the power of the tongue," according to Proverbs 18:21*, then it is imperative that we guard our words, and form the habit of always making a positive confession. Just as a positive confession in harmony with God's

Word will bring blessing and victory, conversely a negative confession of doubt, fear, sickness, or defeat will result in adversity and failure, for the Scriptures declare that you can be *"snared with the words of thy mouth" (Prov. 6:2)*. Satan will keep you bound, poor, sick, and oppressed by ensnaring you with your own words when you make such negative confessions as:

- **"I'm afraid I just cannot do this work as I should."**

- **"I know that I will fail if I try."**

- **"I don't feel too well. I believe I am trying to take the flu."**

- **"I probably will not be able to go, as I am sure that I will not have the money in time."**

- **"I still have my symptoms and pain although I receive prayer for healing several weeks ago. Perhaps it is not God's will to heal me this time."**

- **"No matter how hard I try, it seems I just can- not overcome this problem."**

- **"I wonder if I will ever feel any better."**

- **"I just knew it would rain today; it always does when we plan anything for outdoors."**

- "I've prayed for my wife's salvation, but if any- thing she seems to be getting worse. I just don't think she will ever change."

- "I think that I am taking my husband's cold."

- "Why does this always have to happen to me?"

- "My husband always drives through heavy traffic for me, as I am afraid that I might have an accident."

- "I wonder if this pain in my chest could indicate heart disease."

- "Please do not ask me to speak in public, as I always become quite nervous and cannot testify."

- "My sinus condition always gets worse about this time of the year."

- "I cannot eat this meat because pork always makes me ill."

- "I don't dare attempt that particular task, as it is beyond my ability."

- "We will try to come if things work out, but the prospect isn't too promising."

- **"I don't know what we will do if the cost of living keeps going up."**

- **"I failed to get that important promotion I had hoped for; but it is just as I expected, as I never seem to succeed at anything."**

- **"Well, I made it to work, but that is about all I can say. The way I feel I certainly don't expect to get much done."**

The influence of the powers of darkness upon the human race is nowhere more clearly seen than in Satan's control and influence of man's mind and his confession. Generally, all you ever hear, whether over the radio or TV, on the plane, or in a restaurant, has a negative emphasis. The newspapers and commentators seldom present a good report, as this seems to have no new value. Have you ever heard, for example, that there are about 201,000,000 Americans who are not on drugs? Was the fact reported that thousands of denominational Christians received the baptism in the Holy Spirit and spoke in tongues last year? Were you informed through the news media that there were millions of college students who were not involved in any form of campus rebellion, or revolt against authority last semester? Was it reported in the press that there were over 90,000,000 men who were not involved in any major crimes in the United States in the past 12 months? Did the last conversation you overheard in the restaurant where you ate edify you, or was it the usual negative report of the speaker's recent operation, his peptic ulcers, his accident, or his financial distress? When was the last time anyone complimented, or reported to you any good news concerning some friend or acquaintance about whom they were speaking? Why is it we usually receive a complete medial history concerning all the pains and afflictions of most individuals when we simply address them with the friendly greeting, "How are you today?" On every hand I find the Christians are being defeated by their negative confession. No one would intentionally invite a doctor to inject flu germs directly into his bloodstream; and yet this is precisely what you do when you confess that you believe that you are taking the flu at the first symptom, for the Scriptures declare, *"thou art snared with the words of thy mouth" (Prov. 6:2)*. Your condition will always parallel your confession. The Word of God tells us why: *"For as he thinketh in his heart, so is he" (Prov. 23:7)*, and *"out of the abundance of the heart the mouth speaketh" (Mt. 12:34)*. If you think you will fail—you will. If you say you can't—then you can't. If you confess you are sick—you will be sick. If you say you cannot overcome the problem—then you can- not. If you confess that you will be defeated— you will. Why? It is because you will generally experience what you think and confess. It has taken medical science thousands of years to learn this truth, which God revealed to Israel in the time of Solomon, that we actually precondition our lives for sickness or health, prosperity or adversity, by what we think and say. As we have already pointed out, the medical authorities tell us today that most physical illness is psychosomatic; that is, it results from wrong thinking, worry, and emotional stress. For instance, how we think we feel and what we confess about it has a definite effect upon how we actually feel. Jesus came to give us an abundant life—a life free from sin, sickness, poverty, fear, depression, worry, and defeat. However, most Christians have allowed Satan to rob them of their joy and peace, as well as their health and prosperity, through his influence upon their thoughts and their consequent confession. The average Christian keeps his mind and speech so cluttered with negatives and doubts that he has forfeited almost all hope and expectation for anything better, and has accepted a certain amount of poverty, sickness, and failure as inevitable. In order to rise above all these opposing circumstances and walk in victory with our inheritance restored, we must change our thinking habits, and speech. It is then that we shall begin to experience the dynamic power of a positive confession. People reveal the nature and extent of their faith by what they say or confess. What you confess is your faith speaking, and will reveal whether or not your faith is strong, weak, great, or small. Since you generally receive what you confess (Mk. 11:23; Prov. 18:21), then if your confession agrees with the Word of God you will receive what He has promised. A true confession of faith always agrees with God's Word, for this is the meaning of the Greek term which is translated "to confess" in the New Testament. The literal meaning is "to agree with," or

81

"to speak the same language." If you confess what God's Word says about your sins (1John. 1:9), then you receive forgiveness; and, in the same manner, if you confess what His Word says about your diseases (Ps. 103:3; James 5:14-15), you will receive healing. If, however, you say, "I prayed for the healing of my ulcers, but there are still certain foods that I would not dare eat as I know they would make me ill," then you cannot expect to be healed by faith, for your confession does not agree with God's Word. The Scriptures declare that *"by His stripes ye were healed" (1 Pet. 2:24)*; God's Word states, further- more, that you are to believe that you have received the answer to your petition when you pray. Thus, any confession that does not harmonize with what the Scriptures say will in- variably nullify the Word of God on your behalf. It is important to see that you will never rise above the level of your confession. Your condition or circumstances always tend to parallel your confession. On several occasions I have prayed for the healing of Christians with identical illnesses in some meeting where I would be speaking, in which one would later receive the manifestation of his healing, while the other individual did not. As often as not the cause for failure was clear—either this individuals daily confession concerning his condition was not in agreement with God's Word, or else he did not maintain his confession of faith without doubting until the healing was manifested. Some individuals who lack instruction in the Scriptures concerning the importance of maintaining a positive confession, even in the face of symptoms or contradictory circumstances, will ask, "But isn't this being dishonest to say that I am healed when I still have my pain and symptoms?" Or they ask, "Isn't such a confession just mental suggestion"? No. On the contrary, it is never dishonest to confess about your condition what the Scriptures tell you to say. It is not mere suggestion, but a confession of God's Word when you confess your belief that God has heard and answered your petition when you pray (Mk. 11:24; 1 John. 5:14-15). The reason God requires us to confess, not what we feel or see, but what His Word promises us, is because our condition and circumstances generally remain on about the same level of our confession, for *"death and life are in the power of the tongue" (Prov. 18:21).* I always encourage people to make a positive confession of what the Scriptures have to say about their condition or problem, in spite of what their feelings, symptoms, or the circumstances may imply to the contrary, for Satan's power to afflict or oppress increases or decreases in direct proportion to the positive or negative nature of one's confession. I remind the individual who finds it difficult to understand how that he can maintain a positive confession of healing when he does not feel healed, and his symptoms seem to indicate the contrary, that after successful surgery a patient's condition is medically cured, and al- though he is on the road to recovery, he never feels better for a few days after surgery. Nevertheless, he both believes and confesses what the doctors tell him about his condition, in spite of his contrary feelings, his pain, and his symptoms. However, when the

Heavenly Physician tells him to believe and confess the same thing about his condition after prayer for healing, the average Christian will, if his symptoms do not immediately improve, not only begin to confess what he feels, but will also search the Scriptures for alleged proof-texts in an attempt to justify his sickness and pain. God clearly tells us what He will do for us in His Word, and from that point on He deals with us on the basis of what we say and do about His promises. If, after claiming some promise in His Word, we then begin to express doubt or make some negative confession concerning the situation, this will nullify His Word on our behalf. The importance of our confession is to be seen in Jesus warning that *"by thy words thou shalt be justified, and by thy words thou shalt be condemned" (Mt. 12:37).* Who do you think determines whether or not you can have the abundant life of health, prosperity, joy, victory, and fruitfulness which Jesus promised? God? No. He tells you that with Him there is "no respect or person," and that His promises and blessings are for every believer alike. Is it Satan? No. The Scriptures tell you to "resist the devil and he will flee from you," and that God has given His people "power over all the power of the enemy." Moreover, God admonishes Christians to "give no place to the devil." This means that Satan can have no place in your life unless you grant it to him. No, he is not the one who determines whether you suffer adversity and failure. Your circumstances merely provide you with the opportunity to reveal the extent of your faith in the promises of God. Circumstances in themselves cannot cause victory nor defeat, for Jesus promised that "if ye have faith as a grain of mustard seed, nothing shall be impossible unto you." Who then determines whether or not you enjoy the abundance life promised you? It is you yourself. Are you aware that as you begin each day it is you- and you alone- who will determine the nature of the day you will have, as well as its outcome? Were you aware that you have been given the choice of deciding whether or not you will be happy or sad, sick or well, worried or calm, victorious or defeated? I have never been able to understand why, when God has promised to heal, protect, deliver, and provide all our needs abundantly, telling us again and again that the choice between blessing and adversity lies within our own hands *"all things, whatsoever, ye shall ask in prayer, believing, ye shall receive," (Mt. 21:22)*, that the majority of Christians will choose unhappiness, sickness, poverty, and trouble day after day. It is the result of negative thinking and a negative confession. Everyone preconditions his life by what he thinks, believes, and confesses. Insurance companies know, for example, that some people are poor insurance risks because they are "accident prone." They fear that they may have an accident, and then begin to express their fears, and as a consequence they often experience what they believe and confess. Most of the people who got the flu last winter did so because they confessed that they would at the first sign of a symptom, saying, "I think I must be getting the flu." Many people are dying prematurely of coronary disease because they are confessing such fears as a result of reading the medical reports on the dangers of cholesterol, as well as the insurance statistics concerning the average life-span of the American population. Medical science informs us that a large percentage of all illness stems from emotional stress resulting from wrong attitudes, negative thoughts, and anxiety, as well as from a negative confession concerning these things. Chris- tians are often in poverty, or are financially burdened, because they are confessing that they never really expect to get out of debt. Many Christians are sick and afflicted, some are neurotic, and others are suffering nervous collapse, or heart failure, because they have never learned that "as a man thinketh in his heart, so is he," and that "death and life are in the power of the tongue." In Hebrew 3:1, Jesus is called the High Priest of our confession. This means that as our High Priest he can act in our behalf to save, bless, heal, protect, and deliver us, if we give Him a positive confession which is in harmony with the Word of God. However, a confession of doubt or fear concerning our situation or need hinders His ministry on our behalf, and opens a channel of access for Satan to enter and oppress. "How are you today?" someone asks a fellow-Christian as he enters the door of the church. "I'm not feeling too well. I believe I'm trying to take a cold. It seems that I usually do at the first opportunity," he replied, determined that he is going to allow Satan to afflict him with it if at all possible. The question, "How are you?" is merely a friendly greeting, no an invitation to in- form the inquirer of your symptoms and problems, or to confess that Satan has the victory over you. The Scriptures show that sickness or health, prosperity or adversity, are directly related to our confession. Therefore, it is important to know, for instance, when illness strikes that there are three factors to consider if healing is to be obtained. First, there is what God says about our affliction *"He healeth all our disease," (Ps. 103:3);* secondly, there is what Satan says about the situation "you are sick"; "you may die"; "don't be foolish and rely on prayer alone"; "obtain medical treatment as this is serious"; and thirdly, there is what you confess about your condition. This is why what you say determines the outcome, for you have the choice of agreeing either with your adversary (the devil), or with God. In Revelation 12:10 Satan is called "the accuser of the brethren, who stands before the throne of heaven accusing us day and night"; whereas Jesus is designated as our Advocate (1 John. 2:1), and the High Priest of our confession (Heb. 3:1), who pleads our case without ceasing before the Father. What is Jesus pleading on our behalf with? Two things: with His blood, and with our confession. For Satan, we are informed, is overcome by the blood of the Lamb, and with the word of our testimony (Rev. 12:11). As the High Priest of our confession Jesus is pleading our defense against Satan's accusations, not only with His precious blood, but also with our testimony (what we say). Thus, when you say, "I don't feel well; I must be coming down with something"; when you say, "I'm afraid I can- not do this or that, as I don't believe that I have the ability"; when you say, "I won't be able to afford it"; when you say, "I have prayed for my healing, but I am beginning to wonder if I will ever get well"; when you say, "I've tried and tried, but I just can't seem to overcome this problem"; when you say, "this situation seems impossible, or the solution appears hopeless," then you have joined your confession with that our your Accuser, Satan. As a result Jesus Christ cannot act as your High Priest on the basis of such a negative confession of doubt, fear, or failure. He can only act as the High Priest of a good confession. Giving your accuser the fiery darts with which to wound you, for you will find that you have been snared by the words of your own mouth (Prov. 6:2). The victorious life is based upon a positive confession of the four Biblical truths. A positive affirmative of these facts will compel Satan to acknowledge your authority and victory over him. This will in turn have the effect of breaking the enemy's power to bind, hinder, and oppress you. God expects us to confess (1) what we are in Christ; (2) where we are in Christ; (3) what we possess in Christ; and (4) what we can do in Christ.

I.

CONFESS WHAT YOU ARE IN CHRIST (YOUR STANDING).

What do the Scriptures say that we now are in Christ? We are informed in II Corinthians 5:17 that *"If any man be in Christ, he is a new creature: old things are passed away; behold, all things are become new."* Now, when we are told that "old things are passed away," and that "all things are become new," we are not to limit this merely to the passing away of our sins, but the atonement includes also the removal of our disease and pain, as well as deliverance from anxiety, worry, poverty, oppression and defeat. When God promises us that all things have become new, then He expects us to confess this fact—that we have been liberated and renewed in mind, body, soul, and spirit, for our circumstances and condition will never rise above the level of what we believe we are in Christ. The Scriptures declare that "ye are complete in him" (Col. 2:10), that you have been liberated from the "power of darkness" (Col. 1:13), as well as the effects of the curse (Gal. 3:13), and that you are now sons of God and joint-heirs with Christ (Gal. 4:6-7). The victorious life is based upon our continual confession of our present standing in Christ.

II

CONFESS WHERE YOU ARE IN CHRIST

Many Christians are living a life of oppression and defeat at the hands of the enemy, because they do not know where they now are in Christ–their position in Him. They believe they have been crucified with Christ (Gal. 2:20); they believe they have died with Christ (II Cor. 5:14); they believe that they have risen with Christ (Col. 3:11); but they are unable to walk in victory as they should, triumphant over the powers of darkness, because they do not know that they have also ascended into the heavens with Christ, and are seated with Him "far above all principality, and power, and might, and dominion" (Eph. 1:21). God has not called us to contend with Sa- tan for a place of victory, but to overcome him from our position of victory which we already have in Christ. Jesus tells us that He has given us authority over all the power of the enemy (Lk. 10:17-19), and that all power in heaven and earth has been given unto Him, which He in turn has committed unto us (Mt. 28:18-20; Mk. 16:17-20). Too many Christians today are like the elder brother in the Parable of the Prodigal Son, who, ignorant of his position, confessed that he had nothing, and that his wayward brother had greater rights and privileges than he, until his father re- minded him of his position as a son, and that all he had to do to obtain what he desired was to confess his position and his rights to it. The prodigal son was more a son in actual practice than his elder brother, for he came to himself, rose up from his position of poverty where he was glad to eat the—husks,‖ returned to his father, and was restored to his position as a son and heir. Believers today need to —come to themselves‖ and rise up from their position of defeat, where they are barely existing on the —husks‖ or religion, and return to their Father, once more claiming their position as the sons of God. Victory will not be yours until you believe it and confess that it belongs to you. Until you accept on faith the declaration in God's Word that you have also ascended with Christ, and are now seated with Him in a position of power and authority, Satan will continue to exercise his power over your life. Boldly confess that you no longer need to contend with Satan for a place of victory, but that you shall overcome him from a position of victory at the throne of God. The Christian has this authority by virtue of his relationship to Christ, but we must first claim and confess our authority over Satan before we can effectively command him to obey. We have been authorized by virtue of our heavenly position to put up a bold resistance in the Name of Jesus Christ against the powers of darkness, and we have been assured that they must obey!

III

CONFESS WHAT YOU ARE IN CHRIST (YOUR STANDING)

Satan keeps most Christians in bondage to some degree at least because they do not know, or claim, what belongs to them as the result of their inheritance in Christ. As a consequence they have allowed the Enemy to usurp their rights and privileges, and to rob them of their healing, health, joy, and peace. Christians are rich spiritually, materially, and physically, but too few are aware of the fact, believing instead that they are not to receive any of their inheritance now, and benefit from it in the present life, but only in the world to come. The Scriptures, on the contrary, declare that the believer's inheritance belongs to him now, for God promises that *"all things are yours . . . whether the world, or life, or death, or things present, or things to come"* (I Cor. *3:21-22)*. God has given us all things in Christ now as joint-heirs with Him (Rom. 8:16-17). The Scriptures are filled with thousands of promises, whereby God has made provision for our every need, both spiritual and temporal, as well as for the

91

accomplishment of the work He has commissioned His Church to do. All these provisions and blessings are available to the extent that we are willing to press through by faith and confess that they are ours now. It is tragic that Satan is able to keep Chris- tians in such bondage because they have not been taught what really belongs to them as joint-heirs with Christ. If the tax appraiser comes to their homes and asks them to declare what goods and personal property they own, they have no difficulty in stating what belongs to them. If a thief attempts to steal their car or wallet, they immediately challenge him, saying, "You cannot take that—it is mine!" And yet they will allow Satan, whom Jesus describes as a thief and a robber (John. 10:10), to rob them of their rights and privileges, and not lift a finger to stop him! Until you confess in faith that all those things which the Scriptures clearly state belong to you are actually yours now, then the Enemy will continue to keep you in scriptural, physical, and temporal bondage, by robbing you of your inheritance and usurping your rights and authority.

IV

CONFESS WHAT YOU CAN DO IN CHRIST (YOUR EMPOWERING AND ABILITY)

Frequently we hear Christians confessing what they cannot do. We hear them say, for in- stance, "I'm afraid I cannot do that, as I lack training or the ability"; "I cannot overcome the problem"; "I just can't seem to receive my healing";" I've tried and tried, but I have not been able to receive the baptism in the Holy

Spirit"; "I just cannot seem to get out of debt regardless of how hard I work at it"; "I cannot get along with my employer"; "I cannot get out to the meetings this week"; "I cannot eat certain fried foods as they make me ill"; "I may have to leave the service early as I don't feel too well"; "I just can't get the victory in this matter"; and so on. Sound familiar? It should, inasmuch as this all too frequently is the character of the confessions many Christians are making. One thing is certain—you will never be able to do more than you are willing to confess that you can do in Christ, for *"thou art snared with the words of thy mouth" (Prov. 6:2)*. To walk in victory you should never confess that you cannot do something, or that anything impossible, for the Scriptures say that you should always confess, *"I can do all things through Christ which strengtheneth me" (Phil. 4:13)*. When Moses insisted on confessing that he could not speak to Pharaoh, then he could not, and God was compelled to send Aaron his brother to speak for him (Exdous 4). Peter began to sink when he confessed that he could not stand on the very water which he had been walking on. The Israelites perished in the wilderness because they confessed that they would (Num. 14:1-2, 28-29). It is a sin to limit God by a confession of doubt as to your ability and power in Christ, for He clearly promises you that "And these signs shall follow them that believe; In my name shall they cast out devils; they shall speak with new tongues; they shall take up serpents; and if they drink any deadly thing, it shall not hurt them; they shall lay hands on the sick, and they shall recover" (Mk. 16:17-18). Jesus said, *"He that believeth on me, the works that I do shall he do also; and greater works than these shall he do,..." (John. 14:12)*, and promised us that *"if ye have faith as a grain of mustard seed... nothing shall be impossible unto you" (Mt. 17:20)*. Change a negative confession into a positive one, and truly nothing shall be impossible unto you. One woman, for whom I prayed to receive the baptism in the Holy Spirit, said, after several moments of silence as she waited for the Spirit to give her new tongues, "Oh, I just can't speak in tongues. I can't! I can't!" "Don't say,! I can't! I can't! Confess, I can, I can!" was my immediate reply, whereupon she immediately confessed, "I can! I can!" and then found that she could and did. It was her negative confession which had bound her so that the Holy Spirit could not anoint her with utterance in new tongues. Inasmuch as the Scriptures declare that you can be snared by the words of your mouth (Prov. 6:2), and that *"by thy words thou shalt be justified, and by thy words thou shalt be condemned" (Mt. 12:37)*, then it is imperative that we guard our lips from giving expressions to anything negative, which is an open invitation to the Enemy to oppress or overcome us.

V

THE SIX-FOLD SECRET OF A POSITIVE CONFESSION

God deals with us on the basis of what we say or confess, according to Matthew 12:34-37. In Mark 11:23 Jesus promises us that we shall receive whatsoever we say. We are informed in Romans 10:10 that confession is the means by which we obtain possession of that which we believe, while Proverbs 18:21 declares that *"death and life are in the power of the tongue."* The reason that the Scriptures place such an emphasis upon a positive confession is because we shall never rise above the level of our confession, for our condition and circumstances generally parallel our confession. If we pray concerning some need and then express doubt as to the outcome, we shall receive nothing. If we confess sickness when certain symptoms occur, then we shall be sick, for by the law of confession sickness confessed is sickness possessed. When you claim deliverance from some form of financial distress and then, instead of resting in the confidence that God will supply your needs according to His promise (Phil 4:19), you confess anxiety, or you begin to consider what you will do in the event the money does not come, you will nullify God's promise on your behalf. Inasmuch as the Scriptures inform us that we shall receive whatever we confess, then, if we desire to walk in victory 365 days a year, we must form the habit of making a positive confession when we speak. How is this accomplished?

THE SECRET OF A POSITIVE CONFESSION IS SIX-FOLD.

1. First, you must set a watch on your lips, and guard your mind.

If we expect to walk in health, prosperity, and victory, then we must, first of all, pray as David, *"Set a watch, O Lord, before my mouth; keep the door of my lip" (Ps. 141:3)*, confessing also with him, *"I will take heed to my ways, that I sin not with my tongue: I will keep my mouth with a bridle" (Ps. 39:1)*. In order to develop a positive confession it is necessary to see that we must first learn how to be quiet, before we attempt to learn how to speak effectively. As infants we struggled, slowly learning how to speak; more- over, we have spent years developing our vocabulary, only to discover that much of what we have learned must be unlearned, as it is a primary cause for much of our problems and failure, as well as our sicknesses and infirmities. Much of what the average person talks about or confesses is negative and does not edify either himself or others. The Scriptures admonish us, *"Let no corrupt communication proceed out of your mouth, but that which is good to the use of edifying, that it may minister grace unto the hearers" (Eph. 4:29)*. We must eliminate certain expressions from our thoughts and speech, as most people have their minds and speech so cluttered with negatives that they are robbing themselves of their health, happiness, prosperity, and victory. The Lord admonishes us to stop confessing our doubts, symptoms, and fears, as well as our uncertainties, and to *"be still and know that I am God" (Ps. 46:10)*. In Ecclesiastes 5:2 He warns us: *"Be not rash with thy mouth, and let not thine heart be hasty to utter anything before God . . . therefore let thy words be few."* A positive confession begins with sanctified silence. Learning how to be quiet, and speaking only those things which edify both us and others is the secret of a positive confession. Likewise, you should refuse entrance into your mind anything of a negative, contrary, resentful, or depressive nature. Guard your heart and mind, for this is the place the Enemy usually attempts to work, as he knows you will generally confess what you think and believe, for *"... for out of the abundance of the heart the mouth speaketh." (Matt.12:34)* Failure to guard your mind against Satan's depressive and negative suggestions is one of the major causes for much of the Christian's fear, oppression, sickness, and defeat. Therefore, we admonished to *"Keep thy heart with all diligence; for out of it are the issues of life" (Prov. 4:23)*. There is a continual warfare going on between God and Satan for the control of your mind and thoughts. If Satan can gain the ascendancy here, then he knows that he can determine what you will say and confess which in turn will affect the course of events in your life. In this way he is able to limit or destroy your effectiveness in the Kingdom of God. The secret of a positive confession is then, first of all, to set a watch on your lips, and guard the door of your mind.

2. Never confess doubt, or anything of a negative nature.

Admitting doubt, even in a small way, will paralyze faith and withhold from you God's blessings (James 1:6-7). You must absolutely refuse to confess doubt, fear, defeat, or anything of a negative nature. We have found time and again that Christians often talk themselves out of their faith, as well as the answer to their prayers, by what they say or confess after claiming some promise from God's Word. One of the greatest causes for defeat in the lives of Christians is the tongue. A negative confession, or a confession of doubt, is your own ad- mission that you are defeated and that Satan has the victory. Never allow yourself to use negative or doubtful expressions of speech, for it is a luxury which you cannot afford to indulge in. Develop a vocabulary of faith from God's Word. You must refuse moreover to listen to the doubts of others as this can adversely affect your own confession of faith. Listening to the doubts, disbelief, skepticism, and the uncertainties of others can seriously undermine or weaken your own faith. Never discuss the problems which you have committed to the Lord, or God's promises you have claimed by faith, with those who do not believe that God positively answers every prayer of faith based upon His Word. For example, if by faith you have claimed healing from some illness, Satan often seeks to use the unbelief and skepticism of others to implant doubts in your own heart. Many of his tares are sown in just this way, and as a result the seed of God's Word is choked and be- comes unfruitful. It is also possible to forfeit healing once obtained by faith if you allow doubt to affect your faith. We are personally acquainted with instances where this has occurred.

3. Harmonize your confession with God's.

God deals with us on the basis of what we say or confess. You can easily confirm this for yourself by determining to bring your confession into harmony, not with what you feel or see, not with what others may say, or with what the circumstances might appear to be, but into agreement with the Word of God. Study, and then begin to confess the promises of such Scriptures as, for example, Exodus 15:26; Psalms 37:91; 103:1-5; 121; Matthew 6:33; 18:19; 21:22; Mark 11:22-24; Romans 8:28; 1 Corinthians 3:21-22; II Corinthians 1:20; Philippians 4:13, 19; Hebrew 13:6; James 1:2-4; and 3 John 2. These are just a few of the countless promises God makes to the believer, which, if faithfully confessed, will enable you to live victoriously 365 days a year. Keep in mind that the term translated "to confess" (homologeo) means in the New Testament Greek, "to agree with," or "to speak the same language." Your confession must agree with God's (i.e., agree with what He has said in His Word), if you are to receive an answer from Him. If you say, "I prayed for the healing of my heart condition, and I hope that God will heal me some time, if it is His will", you cannot expect to receive healing on such a confession. Why? Simply because it is out of agreement with what God has confessed about your physical illness, for He has said that *"...by His stripes ye were healed" (1 Pet. 2:24)*, that *"the prayer of faith shall save the sick" (James 5:15)*, that He *"healeth all thy diseases" (Ps. 103:3)*, and that *"what things soever ye desire, when we pray, believe that ye receive them, and ye shall have them" (Mk. 11:24)*. A positive confession is to extend even to our praying, or we cannot expect God to answer our prayers. God never works in advance of the level of your faith, for your faith is the channel through which He works to answer your prayers. God's answers always keep pace with your confession. Therefore, you are not to confess what you feel and see, or what the circumstances may appear to be, but confess what God has said in His Word. Never expect God to bless you in spite of your negative confession, for He has promised to help those who are willing to confess in faith what He has said and promised to do (1 John. 5:14-15).

4. Confess victory before you see it.

Gideon and his small band of 300 men shouted the victory beforehand, and as a result the enemy became so frightened that the Midianites destroyed one another in their confusion. The Israelites did not wait until the walls of Jericho began to crumble, before believing that God had given the city into their hands, but they shouted the walls down by faith. The Apostle Paul tells us in Hebrews 11:1 that "faith is the evidence of things not seen." Faith is not sight. Faith can only operate in the realm of the invisible, concerning those things which we have prayed for, but which we do not yet see manifested to our sight. Here is where most Christians run into difficulty. They have lived so long in the visible realm of the senses that it is difficult for them to believe and confess that they have the answer to their prayers before they see or feel some evidence of it. For instance, frequently we have found that an individual will claim a promise of God for the healing of some ailment, and then if the condition does not seem to improve immediately, he will begin to reason in his mind saying, "Well, I must not be healed, as I do not feel healed, inasmuch as I still have my symptoms." Moreover, he is even more firmly convinced, upon looking at his appearance in the mirror, that God has not answered his petition. However, we must see that healing never depends upon how we feel, nor on what we see, but entirely upon what we believe and con- fess, for we are told that "as a man thinketh in his heart, so is he," and that "out of the abundance of the heart the mouth speaketh." Until we learn that the manifestation of healing always comes after our confession of healing, then we will be trying to put the effect before the cause. Many Christians are trying to believe with their "eyes" and with their "senses" or "feeling," whereas the Scriptures say that we believe with the "heart" (spirit). We must first believe and sincerely confess in faith that we have received, or we shall never have the answer manifested to our sight. Jesus tells us in Mark 11:24 to believe that we have received when we pray, and then we shall have it (1 John. 5:14-15). We are never to depend upon feelings or appearances, for Satan works through the realm of the senses, and can manipulate the feelings with symptoms and pains, and can also deceive us by what appears to be true to our sight. Appearances can deceive. When Jesus cursed the fig tree His word of faith killed it immediately. Although it did not appear to be dead until later, it was dead nevertheless, in spite of appearances. The sun "appears" to rise and set each day; however, in reality, it is the earth which is turning in relation to the sun, which remains still.

Often when driving, the car begins to "feel" as if a tire is going flat. How often have you stopped to investigate, only to discover that there is nothing wrong. It only felt as if you had a flat tire. On numerous occasions, those for whom I have prayed for healing found that they did not "feel" nor "look" healed immediately after prayer. But in every case where those for whom we pray believe and confess, not what they feel or see, but what the Word of God says (i.e., 1 Pet. 2:24; Mk. 11:24), they find that the manifestation will ultimately come. God often uses bodily processes or our glands, for example, to facilitate healing. It is nonetheless supernatural when He heals in this manner, for it is without the use of medicine or other remedies. In this case he caused the cyst to come to a "head" much as a boil does, thus causing it to drain and leave his system. We have seen this happen in other instances also. Occasionally, after prayer conditions may not seem to improve for a time, or may even appear to get worse, as God works the poison or disease out of the body. Thus, if we rely only upon appearances or feelings, then Satan will deceive us and rob us of our healing. Faith is confessing the victory ahead of time; it is confessing that you have your answer when you pray, believing that God will give the manifestation in due time as He promises to do (Heb. 10:23, 35-36; Num. 23:19). You are only entitled to that which you bodily confess is already yours by virtue of God's faithfulness.

5. Hold fast to your confession of faith without wavering.

Often things will look no different after you claim some promise and confess your faith in it. It is at this point that you must be very careful to guard your confession, as Satan, who is a deceiver, will try to get you to testify to your feelings, symptoms, or circumstances. Once you confess a promise of God, absolutely refuse to take a word of your confession back, regardless of the circumstances, or how long you must wait for the manifestation of the answer. Why? We are told in Hebrews 10:23, *"Let us hold fast the profession of our faith without wavering; for he is faithful that promise."* We are to maintain a daily, constant confession of faith in the promise we have claimed until it is manifested. Many can believe a promise and claim it in prayer, but if the answer is not manifested soon enough, they begin to waver and doubt, giving up their confession of faith. As a result they receive nothing. Healing, for instance, is always in response to a confession of faith, but a confession that can only persevere for a day, week, or a month, is not a healing confession. Many fail to receive what they ask from God because they cannot keep up confession without wavering in the midst of trial, testing, pain, or symptoms. Sickness often can only be overcome by maintaining a positive confession of God's promise in the face of all apparent evidence to the contrary. When you claim healing, you have thereby challenged Satan's right to oppress you. You have, as it were, entered his domain, and a battle often ensues. He will contest every inch of ground which you claim. Often he will not withdraw his symptoms until the last moment that God allows him, as he knows from past experience that if he can maintain his hold long enough he can ultimately discourage most Christians and break their confessions of faith. This is why a constant confession of faith in the promise of God will eventually overcome Satan's oppression and he will have to release his hold on you and vacate the premises. Satan's power to afflict and oppress in- creases or decreases in direct proportions to your confession of faith in the Word of God which you have claimed. When Satan discovers you have learned the secret of using God's Word to overcome him (Rev. 12:11), he will eventually be forced to re- lease his hold on you, or on your circumstances. But often he will not withdraw until he has exhausted his resources in an attempt to break your confession of faith in the integrity of the Word of God. He will try to implant fear and doubt into your mind to confuse you; at times he will cause persecution to come upon you for your faith; on occasion he will oppress you with new symptoms and pain, or cause the old ailment to appear to return; he will, if possible, surround you with contradictory advice from your friends, or will cause your family to think that you have become a religious fanatic because of your stand on the Word. But he knows your confession, if maintained with- out wavering, will ultimately defeat him and his work in your life; therefore, *"let us hold fast the profession of our faith without wavering; for he is faithful that promised," and "cast not away therefore your confidence, which hath great recompense of reward. For ye have need of patience, that after ye have done the will of God, he might receive the promise" (Heb. 10:23, 35-36).*

6. If Satan tempts you to doubt, boldly take the initiative away from him.

As we have seen, frequently after claiming some promise in God's Word, Satan will challenge your decision, and you may find yourself undergoing a period of trial. If, for example, you have claimed a promise of healing for some physical ailment, Satan will attempt to get your attention on your symptoms in an effort to cause you to doubt and break your confession of faith in God's promise. In such instances, a bold reaffirmation of your faith in God's Word when tempted to doubt will generally kill doubt at the roots. Holding fast to your confession of faith without wavering (Heb. 10:23) is a defensive measure whereby you keep faith in the promise of God until the manifestation of the answer; however, it is also necessary many times, especially during a period of trial, to take offensive measures against the powers of darkness. There will be times when you must boldly move deeper into Satan's territory by faith when he challenges your confession. When Goliath threatened David, saying, "I will give thy flesh unto the fowls of the air, and to the beasts of the field," David immediately replied, "And I will smite thee, and take thine head from thee!" When the giant then arose and drew nigh to meet him, instead of re- treating in fear, we are told that

"David hasted, and ran toward the army to meet the Philistine" *(1 Sam.17:44).* When the Enemy comes against you and challenges your faith in some unusual way, then instead of retreating in doubt and fear as many so often do, like David advance against him and act your faith, boldly reaffirming your confidence in God's Word, as well as your authority over the powers of darkness. We are told to "resist the devil, and he will flee from you." When Satan advances one step against you in an effort to break your confession of faith—resist him in faith, and boldly advance two steps against him, and the Scriptures assure you that *"he will flee from you."*

I.

PREPARATION AFFIRMATIONS

"I ACCEPT JOY, POWER, LOVE, HAPPINESS, MONEY, ABUNDANCE, AND GOOD HEALTH INTO MY LIFE."

I thank God my invisible source. "I accept joy, power, love, happiness, money, abundance, and good health into my life." They are already mine, and come to me in a safe and loving way, according to divine will and the free will of all concerned. And so it is.

"I ACCEPT A NEW LOVING ATTITUDE, AND JOY-FULLY RECEIVE ALL THE BLESSINGS OF GOD."

I thank God, my invisible source. "I accept a new loving attitude, and joyfully receive all the blessings of God." They are already mine, and come to me in a safe and loving way, according to divine will and free will of all concerned And so it is.

"ALL THE MONEY I NEED TO PAY OFF MY CURRENT CREDIT CARD DEBT COMES TO ME NOW."

"All the money I need to pay off my current credit card debt comes to me now." I thank God, which is already mine and comes to me in a safe and loving way, according to divine will and the free will of all concerned. And so it is.

ATTRACTION

Today, I attract all that I need to create abundance in my life. The power is within me.

BALANCE AND FLOW

My entire energy is in balance and harmony with all of life. I flow with the process of life, and all of its events and happenings strengthen me.

CHANGE

Change is normal. I cope with the changes life has to offer easily and without struggle.

EGO

My ego is healthy and vital, and under control.

FEAR AND DOUBT

I recognize that, at times, I am fearful. At that moment, I breathe deeply and ask the Holy Spirit for guidance. Fear is a figment of my imagination. From now on, I choose only joy and fulfillment. I face my life without fear or doubt.

INTUITION

I pay more attention to my intuition than my logical mind, because it is always accurate.

POSITIVE ENERGY

Each day I create positive energy, circumstances, and events.

PROBLEMS

I allow my problems to work themselves out with- out pain and struggle.

RECEIVING

I am ready and open to receive my desires. I am in the perfect place and have all that it takes to accomplish my goals. I create all that I need and want. Everything comes easy to me. I am living in a constant state abundance. I am open and ready for the abundance of the universe to manifest in my life.

SPIRITUAL GOALS

It is easy for me to set spiritual goals. I am clear in my mind that all that occurs or will occur in my life has spiritual meaning. As I set goals for my spiritual growth, I am confident they will be achieved.

STRUGGLE

All forms of struggle are released from my consciousness and my life. All is well and working in my highest good.

WISDOM

I am wise and make sound choices. My knowledge, skills, and talents help to make this lifetime a loving, abundant, prosperous, and fulfilling one.

ASSURANCE OF HEALING

I know that Jesus took my infirmities and bared my sicknesses. My healing was provided for me in the atonement. By His stripes I am healed.

ASSURANCE OF WEALTH

I know that it's the Lord my God that gives me power to get wealth. I know that our Lord Jesus Christ became poor, that through His poverty, I might become rich. The wealth of the wicked is being stored up for me.

II.

MANIFESTING AFFIRMATION

CAR PURCHASE

I am the proud owner of a brand new car. This (you may add the model, year, make, color, etc., if you like or just insert the word "car")_____ comes to me now.

CONFIDENCE

I exude confidence. I face all situations with poise and grace. My self-confidence and faith in my ability is strong and never wavers.

FINANCIAL INDEPENDENCE

I am financially independent. All the money I need is mine, exactly when I need it. I have all the money I will ever need or want.

III.

PRACTICAL EXAMPLES

I. Positive confession and prayer

Prayer is the formulation of an idea concerning something we wish to accomplish. Prayer is the soul's sincere desire. Your desire is your prayer. It comes out of your deepest needs, and it reveals the things you want in life. That is the real nature of prayer, the effective expression of life's hunger and thirst for peace, harmony, health, joy, and all the other blessings of life.

II. The following are some examples of effective prayer and confession:

a) *Do this prayer- confession several times a day:*

I like money. I use it wisely, constructively, and judiciously. Money is constantly circulating in my life. I release it with joy and it returns to me multi- plied in a wonderful way. It is good and very good Money flows to me in avalanches of abundance. I use it for good only, and I am grateful for my good and for the riches of my mind.

b) *Let this be your daily affirmation; write it in your heart:*

I am one with the infinite riches of my spirit. It is my right to be rich, happy, and successful. Money flows to me freely, copiously, and endlessly. I am forever conscious of my true worth, I give of my talents freely, and I am wonderfully blessed financially. It is wonderful.

c) *The infinite intelligence of my spirit is all wise.*

(This prayer is for those who are looking to buy a home)

My Human Spirit reveals to me the ideal home that meets all the requirements and that I can afford. I am now turning this request over to my spirit. I know it responds according to the nature of my request with absolute faith and confidence in the same way that a farmer deposits a seed in the ground, trusting implicitly in the laws of growth.

d) The creative intelligence of my spirit knows what is best for me.

Its tendency is always lifeward, and it reveals to me the right decision, which blesses me and all concerned. I give thanks for the answer that I know will come to me.

IV

SLEEP IN PEACE AND WAKE IN JOY

a) If you suffer from insomnia, you will find the following prayer very effective:

Repeat it slowly, quietly, and lovingly prior to sleep. My toes are relaxed, my ankles are relaxed, my abdominal muscles are relaxed, my heart and lungs are relaxed, my hands and arms, my necks are relaxed, my brain is relaxed, my face is relaxed, my eyes are relaxed, my whole body and mind are relaxed. I fully and freely forgive every- one, and I sincerely wish for them harmony, health, peace and all the blessing of life. I am at peace; I am poised, serene, and calm. I rest in security and in peace. A great stillness steals over me, and a great calm quiets my whole being as I know and realize the Divine Presence within me. I know that the realization of life and love heals me. I wrap myself in the mantle of love and fall asleep filled with goodwill for all. Throughout the night peace remains with me, and in the morning I shall be filled with life and love. A circle of love is drawn around me. I will fear no evil, for thou art with me. I sleep in peace, I wake in joy, and in Him I live, move, and have my being.

b) *The infinite intelligence within that gave me this desire* leads guides and reveals to me the perfect plan for the unfolding of my desire. I know the deeper wisdom of my spirit is now responding, and what I feel and claim within is expressed in the without. There is a balance, and equilibrium.

c) *My spirit knows the answer.*
It is responding to me now. I give thanks because I know the infinite intelligence of my spirit knows all things and is revealing the perfect answer to me now. My real conviction is now setting free the majesty and of my spirit. I rejoice that is so.

d) *The perfection of God is now being ex- pressed through me.*
The idea of perfect health is now filling my spirit. The image God has of me is a perfect image; and my spirit is re-creating my

body in perfect accordance with the perfect image held in the mind of God. My body and all its organs were created by God and are being maintained by my spirit. My Human Spirit knows how to heal me. Its infinite wisdom fashions and keeps all my organs, tissues, muscles, and bones functioning. This infinite healing presence within me is now transforming every cell of my being, making me whole and perfect. I give thanks for the healing I know is taking place at this time. Wonderful are the works of the creative intelligence within me.

KEY SCRIPTURE READING

"I call heaven and earth to record this day against you, that I have set before you life and death, blessing and cursing: therefore choose life, that both thou and thy seed may live:
Deut. 30:19

"Beloved, I wish above all things that thou mayest prosper and be in health, even as thy soul prospereth." **III John 2**

CHAPTER SIX

YOUR RIGHT TO BE WEALTHY

The apostle Paul said in II Corinthians 8:9 that Jesus Christ was rich, yet for our sake He be- came poor that through His poverty (the Law of Action and Reaction) we might be rich. In Deuteronomy 8:18 God said, *"But thou shalt remember the Lord thy God: for it is he that giveth thee power to get wealth, that he may establish his covenant which he sware unto thy fathers, as it is his day."* In the tenth chapter and tenth verse of John's Gospel, Jesus said, *"...I am come that they might have life, and that they might have it more abundantly."* Solomon said in Ecclesiastes 5:19, *"Every man also to whom God hath given riches and wealth, and hath given him power to eat thereof,, and to take his portion, and to rejoice in his labour, this is the gift of God."* You have a fundamental right, according to these four scriptures, to be rich. You are here to lead the abundant life and be happy, radiant, and free. You should, therefore, have all the money you need to lead a full, happy, and prosperous life. You are here to grow, expand, and unfold spiritually, mentally, and materially. You have the inalienable right to fully develop and express your- self in all your potentials. An important aspect of that is the ability, should you so choose, to surround yourself with beauty and luxury.

Why be satisfied with just enough to go around when you can enjoy the riches of your Human Spirit? In this chapter, you will learn to make friends with money. Once you do, you will always have all you need and more. Don't let any- one make you feel doubtful or ashamed of your desire to be rich. At its deepest level, it is a desire for a fuller, happier, more wonderful life. It is a cosmic urge. It is not only good, but very good.

MONEY IS A SYMBOL

Money is a symbol of exchange. To you it is a symbol not only of freedom from want, but of beauty, refinement, abundance, and luxury.   It is also a symbol of the economic health of the nation. When your blood is circulating freely in your body, you are healthy. When money is circulating freely in your life, you are economically healthy. When people begin to hoard money, to put it away in tin boxes and become charges with fear, they become economically ill. As a symbol, money has taken many forms throughout the centuries. Almost anything you can think of has served as money at some time and place in history – gold and silver, of course, but also salt, beads, and trinkets of various kinds. In early times people's wealth was often determined by the number of sheep and oxen they owned. Now we use currency and other negotiable instruments. One reason is obvious. It is much more convenient to write a check than to carry a few sheep around with you to pay bills.

HOW TO WALK THE ROYAL ROAD TO RICHES

Once you understand the powers of your Human Spirit, you have within your grasp a road map to the royal road to riches of all kinds – *spiritual, mental, or financial*. Anyone who has taken the trouble to learn the "LAWS OF MIND" and believes knows definitively that he/she will never want. Regardless of economic crises, stock-market fluctuation, recessions, strikes, galloping inflations, or even war, he/she will always be amply supplied. The reason for this is that he/she has conveyed the idea of wealth to his/her spirit. As a result, it keeps them supplied wherever they may be. He/she has convinced himself/herself in their mind that money is forever flowing freely in their lives and that there is always a wonderful surplus available to them. As he/she decrees it, so it is. Should there be a financial collapse tomorrow and every- thing they possesses becomes worthless, they will still attract wealth. They will come through the crisis comfortably and likely even gain advantage from it.

Why You Do Not Have More Money

As you read this chapter, you may be thinking, "I deserve a bigger income than I have." In my opinion, that is true of most people. They really do deserve to have more – but they are not likely to get it. One of the most important reasons these people do not have more money is that they silently or openly condemn it. They refer to money as "filthy lucre." Coupled with this as a reason they do not prosper is that they have a sneaky spirit feeling there is some special (virtue in poverty). This Human Spirit pattern may be due to early-childhood training, or it may be based on false interpretation of scriptures.

MONEY AND A BALANCED LIFE

One time a man came up to me and said, "I am broke. But that's all right. I do not like money. It is the root of all evil". These statements represent the thinking of a confused, neurotic mind. Love of money to the exclusion of everything else will cause you to become "lopsided and unbalanced". You are here to use your power or authority wisely. Some peoples crave power, others crave money If you set your heart on money exclusively and say, "Money is all I want; I am going to give all my attention to amassing money; nothing else matters," you can get money and gain a fortune, but at what cost! Jesus says in Mark 8:36, *"For what, shall it profit a man, if he shall gain the whole world, and lose his own soul?"* Don't ever forget that you are here to lead a balanced life. You must also satisfy the hunger for peace of mind, harmony, love, joy, and perfect health. By making money your sole aim, you made a wrong choice. You thought that was all you wanted, but you found after all your efforts that it was not only the money you needed. No one on his deathbed wishes he had spent more time making money! You also desire true expression of your hidden talents, true place in life, beauty, and the joy of contributing to the welfare and success of others.

119

By learning the laws of your Human Spirit you could have a million dollars or many millions, if you wanted them, and still have peace of mind, harmony, perfect health, and perfect expression.

POVERTY IS A MENTAL ILLNESS

There is no virtue in poverty. It is an illness like any other mental illness. If you were physically ill, you would realize there was some- thing wrong with you. You would seek help and try to cure the condition at once. In the same way, if you do not have enough money constantly circulating in your life, there is something radically wrong with you. The urge of the life principle in you is to- ward growth, expansion, and the life more abundant. You are not here to live in a hovel, dress in rags, and go hungry. You should be happy, prosperous, and successful.

WHY YOU MUST NEVER CRITICIZE MONEY

Here is a simple technique you may use to multiply money in your experience. Use the following statements several times a day. I like money. I use it wisely, constructively, and judiciously. Money is constantly circulating in my life. I release it with joy, and it returns to me multiplied in a wonderful way. It is good and very good. Money flows to me in avalanche. I use it for good only, and I am grateful for my good and for the riches of my mind.

HOW THE SCIENTIFIC THINKER LOOKS AT MONEY

Suppose you discovered a rich vein of gold, silver, lead, copper, or iron in the ground. Would you announce that these things are evil? Of course not! All evil comes from humankind's darkened understanding, from ignorance, from false interpretations of life, and from misuse of the spirit. Since money is simply a symbol, we could just as easily use lead or tin or some other metal as a medium of exchange. In the earlier part of the century, United States dimes and quarters were made from silver. At times, they contained ten cents or twenty-five cents worth of silver. Then the government started making them of cheaper metals. But the worth of a quarter is still twenty- five cents, even if the metal that makes it up is worth far less than that. A physicist will tell you that the only difference between one metal and another is the kind and number of elementary particles in its atoms. If you direct a stream of particles at a block of one metal, you can change it into another. The alchemist's ancient dream of producing gold from baser metals is now within our grasp. But so what? Gold is no more virtuous, or evil, than lead. They are different substances with different properties. It is only because of the long history in which gold was considered especially precious that people love it – or have it – more than they do lead.

OBSTACLES AND IMPEDIMENTS ON THE PATHWAY TO WEALTH

From time to time, you have probably heard someone say, "Anyone who makes a lot of money has to be some kind of crook." This person is creating his own difficulties. Entertaining negative thoughts about those friends and condemning their wealth causes prosperity and wealth to flee. Would you stay with someone who condemns you? Of course not; and neither will wealth. This person is chasing away the thing he is praying for. He is praying in two ways. In one breath he is saying, "I wish wealth to flow to me now." But in the next breath, he is saying, "That fellow's wealth is a dirty, evil thing." This is a contradiction and a signpost on the road to poverty and misery. Always make a special point to rejoice in the wealth of another person.

YOU CANNOT GET SOMETHING FOR NOTHING

In large stores the management hires guards and store detectives to keep people from stealing. Every day they catch a number of people trying to get something for nothing. Anyone who does such a thing is steeped in a mental atmosphere of lack and limitation. In trying to steal from others, they are robbing themselves of peace, harmony, faith, honesty, integrity, goodwill, and confidence. Furthermore, their messages to their Spirit draw to them all manner of loss: loss of character, prestige, social status, and peace of mind. These people do not understand how their minds work. They lack faith in the source of supply. If only they would mentally call on the powers of their Human Spirit and claim that they are guided to their true expression, they would find work and abundance. Then, by honesty, integrity, and perseverance, they would become a credit to themselves and to society at large.

HOW TO USE THE POWER OF YOUR HUMAN SPIRIT FOR WEALTH

If you are having financial difficulties, if you are trying to makes ends meet, it means you have not convinced your Human Spirit that you will always have plenty and some to spare. You know men and women who work a few hours a week and make fabulous sums of money. They do not strive or slave hard. Do not believe the story that the only way you can become wealthy is by the sweat of your brow and hard labor. It is not so; the effortless way of life is the best. Do the thing you love to do, and do it for the joy and thrill of it.

WEALTH IS OF THE MIND

Wealth is ultimately nothing more than a Human Spirit (Consciousness) conviction on the part of the individual. You will not become a millionaire by saying, "I am a millionaire, I am a millionaire." You will grow into a wealth consciousness by building into your mentality the idea of wealth and abundance.

YOUR INVISIBLE MEANS OF SUPPORT

The trouble with most people is that they have no invisible means of support. When business falls away, the stock market drops, or they take a loss on their investments, they seem helpless. The reason for such insecurity is that they do not know how to tap the subconscious mind. They are unacquainted with the inexhaustible storehouse within. Someone with a poverty-type mind finds himself in poverty-stricken conditions. Someone else, with a mind filled with ideas of wealth is sur- rounded by everything he needs. It was never in- tended that we should lead a life of indigence. You can have wealth, everything you need, and plenty to spare. Your words have power to cleanse your mind of wrong ideas and to instill right ideas in their place.

THE IDEAL METHOD FOR BUILDING A WEALTH CONSCIOUSNESS

Perhaps you are saying as you read this chapter, I need wealth and success.‖ This is what you do: Repeat for about five minutes to yourself three or four times a day, "Wealth, Success." These words have tremendous power. They rep- resent the inner power of the Human Spirit. Anchor your mind on this substantial power within you; then conditions and circumstances corresponding to their nature and quality will be manifested in your life. You are not saying, "I am wealthy," you are dwelling on real powers within you. There is no conflict in the mind when you say, "Wealth." Furthermore, the feeling of wealth will well up within you as you dwell on the idea of wealth. The feeling of wealth produces wealth; keep this in mind at all times. Your spirit is like a bank, a sort of universal financial institution. It magnifies whatever you deposit or impress upon it whether it is the idea of wealth or poverty. Choose wealth.

WHY YOUR AFFIRMATIONS FOR WEALTH FAIL

I have talked to many people over the years whose usual complaint is "I have said for weeks and months, "I am wealthy, I am prosperous," and nothing has happened." I discovered that when they said, "I am prosperous, I am wealthy," they felt within that they were lying to themselves. One man told me, "I have affirmed that I am prosperous until I am tired. Things are now worse. I knew when I made the statement that is was obviously not true." His statements were rejected by the Human Spirit, and the opposite of what he outwardly affirmed and claimed was made manifest. Your affirmation succeeds best when it is specific and when it does not produce a mental conflict or argument. The statements made by this man made matters worse because they suggested his lack. Your spirit accepts what you really feel to be true, not just idle words or statements. The dominant idea or belief is always accepted by the Human Spirit.

HOW TO AVOID MENTAL CONFLICT

The following is the ideal way to overcome this conflict for those who have this difficulty. Make this special statement frequently, particularly prior to sleep: "By day and by night I am being prospered in all of my interests." This affirmation will not arouse any argument because it does not contradict you spirit's impression of financial lack.

DON'T SIGN BLANK CHECKS

You sign blank checks when you make such statements as "There is not enough to go around," "There is a shortage," "I will lose the house because I can't meet the mortgage," and so forth. If you are full of fear about the future, you are also writing a blank check and attracting negative conditions to you. Your spirit accepts your fear and negative statement as your request and proceeds in its own way to bring obstacles, delays, lack, and limitation into your life.

YOUR SUBCONSCIOUS GIVES YOU COMPOUND INTEREST

To him that hath the feeling of wealth, more wealth shall be added; to him that hath the feeling of lack, more lack shall be added. Your spirit multiples and magnifies whatever you deposit in it. Every morning as you awaken, deposit thoughts of prosperity, success, wealth, and peace. Dwell upon these concepts. Busy your mind with them as often as possible. These constructive thoughts will find their way as deposits in your spirit and bring forth abundance and prosperity.

TRUE SOURCE OF WEALTH

Your Human Spirit is never short of ideas. There are within it an infinite number of ideas ready to flow into your conscious mind and appear as cash in your pocket in countless ways. This process will continue to go on in your mind regardless of whether the stock market goes up or down, or whether the pound sterling or dollar drops in value. Your wealth is never truly dependent on bonds, stocks, or money in the bank; these are only symbols–necessary and useful, of course, but only symbols. The point I want to emphasize is that you convince your spirit that wealth is yours and that it is always circulating in your life, you will always and inevitably have it, regardless of the form it takes.

TRYING TO MAKE ENDS MEET AND THE REAL CAUSE

There are many people who claim that they are always trying to make ends meet. They seem to have a great struggle to meet their obligations. Have you listened to their conversation? In many instances their conversation runs along this vein. They are constantly condemning those who have succeeded in life and who have raised their heads above the crowd. Perhaps they are saying, "Oh, that fellow has a racket; he is ruthless: he is a crook." This is why they lack. They are constantly condemning the thing they claim to desire and want. The reason they speak critically of their more prosperous associates is because they are envious and covetous of the other's prosperity. The quickest way to cause wealth to take wings and fly away is to criticize and condemn others who have more wealth than you.

A COMMON STUMBLING BLOCK TO WEALTH

There is one emotion that is the cause of the lack of wealth in the lives of many. Most people learn this the hard way. It is envy. For example, if you see a competitor depositing large sums of money in the bank and you have only a meager amount to deposit, does it make you envious? The way to overcome this emotion is to say to self, "Isn't it wonderful! I rejoice in that man's prosperity. I wish for him greater and greater wealth." To entertain envious thoughts is devastating, because it places you in a negative position. Therefore, wealth flows away from you instead of to you. If you are ever annoyed or irritated by the prosperity or great wealth of another, claim immediately that you truly wish for him/her greater wealth in every possible way. This will neutralize the negative thoughts in your mind and cause an ever greater measure of wealth to flow to you by the law of your own Human Spirit.

RUBBING OUT A GREAT MENTAL BLOCK TO WEALTH

If you are worried and critical about some- one who you claim is making money dishonestly, stop worrying about him/her. If your suspicions are correct, you know that such a person is using the law of mind negatively. In time, the law of mind will take care of him/her. Be careful not to criticize them for the reasons previously indicated. Remember: The block or obstacle to wealth is in your own mind. You can now destroy that mental block. This you may do by getting on mental good terms with everyone.

SLEEP AND GROW INTO WEALTH

As you go to sleep at night, practice the following technique. Repeat the word "Wealth" quietly, easily, and feelingly. Repeat over and over again, just like a lullaby. Lull yourself to sleep with the one word, "Wealth." You will be amazed at the result. Wealth should flow to you in avalanches of abundance. This is another example of the Human Spirit power.

KEY SCRIPTURE READING

"Death and Life are in the power of the tongue…"

Proverb 18:21

For as he thinketh in his heart, so is he:…"

Proverb 23:7

"By thy words Thou shalt be justified, and by thy words thou shalt be condemned." Matthew. 12:37

CHAPTER SEVEN

100 POINTS TO REMEMBER

1. **The secret power** is within you. Look within for the answer to your heart's desire.

2. **Your Human Spirit** has the answer to all problems. If you suggest to your spirit prior to sleep, "I want to get up at 6:00 a. m.," it will awaken you at that exact time.

3. Your **Spirit** is the **building** of your body and can heal you. Lull yourself to sleep every night with the idea of perfect health, and your spirit being your faithful servant, will obey you.

4. Every thought is a **cause**, and every condition is an **effect**.

5. You are like a captain navigating a ship. You must give the right orders, or the ship will wreck, the same way, you must give right orders (thoughts and images) to your Human Spirit which controls and govern all your experiences.

6. Never use such expressions as "I can't afford it" or "I can't do this." Your spirit takes you at your word. It sees to it that you do not have the money or the ability to do what you want to do. Affirm, *"I can do all things* through Christ who strengthens me."

7. The **Law of Life** is the **Law of Belief**. A belief is a thought in your mind. Do not believe things that will harm or hurt you. Believe in the power of your spirit to heal, inspire, strengthen, and prosper you. According to your belief it is done unto you.

8. Change your thoughts, and you change your destiny.

9. Think good and good follows. Think evil and evil follows. You are what you think all day long.

10. Your **Human Spirit** does not argue with you. It accepts what your conscious mind decrees. If you say, "I can't afford it," your spirit works to make it true.

11. You have the power to choose. Choose health and happiness, wealth and success. Choose to be friendly, compassionate and loving.

12. Your **Conscious Mind** is the **"watchman at the gate."** Its chief function is to protect your spirit from false impressions. Choose to believe that something good can happen and is happening now. Your greatest power is your capacity to choose. **Choose abundance.**

13. The suggestions and negative confession of others over you have no power to hurt you. The only power is the movement of your own thoughts. You can choose to reject the thoughts or statement of others and affirm the good. You have the power to choose how you will react.

14. Watch what you say. You have to give an account for every idle word. Never say, "I will fail; I will lose my job; I can't pay this bill." Your Spirit cannot take a joke. It brings all these things to pass.

15. Whatever your conscious mind assumes and believes to be true, your **Spirit** will accept and bring to pass. Believe in good fortune, divine guidance, right action, and all the blessings of life.

16. Your spirit controls all the **vital processes** of your body and knows the answer to all problems.

17. Prior to sleep, turn over a specific request to your spirit and prove it's miracle-working power to yourself.

18. Whatever you impress on the spirit man is ex- pressed on the screen of space as conditions, experiences, and events. Therefore, you should carefully watch all ideas and thoughts entertained in your conscious mind.

19. **The Law of Action** and **Reaction** (Law of Reciprocity) is universal. Your thought is action, and the reaction is the automatic response of your spirit to your thought. Watch your thoughts.

20. All frustration is due to unfulfilled desires. If you dwell on obstacles, delays, and difficulties your spirit responds accordingly, and you are blocking your own good.

21. The **Life Principle** will flow through you rhythmically and harmoniously if you consciously affirm: "I believe that my spirit and the Holy Spirit that gave me this desire is now fulfilling it through me." This dissolves all conflicts.

22. You can interfere with the normal rhythm of your heart, lungs, and other organs by worry, anxiety, and fear. Feed

your spirit with thoughts of harmony, health, and peace; and all the functions of your body will become normal again.

23. Keep your **conscious mind** busy with the **expectation** of the best and your spirit will faithfully reproduce your habitual thinking.

24. Imagine the happy ending or solution to your problem; feel the thrill of accomplishment and what you imagine and feel will be accepted by your spirit, which will bring it to pass.

25. Remind yourself frequently that the healing power is in your spirit.

26. Know that faith is like a seed planted in the ground; it grows after its kind. Plant the idea (seed) in your mind, water and fertilize it with expectancy and it will become manifest.

27. All diseases originate in the mind. Nothing appears on the body unless there is a mental pat- tern corresponding to it.

28. The symptoms of almost any disease can be induced in you by hypnotic suggestion. This shows you the power of your thought.

29. There is only one process of healing and that is **faith**. **God** has given to us the **power** to heal within the **Human Spirit**.

30. Develop a definite plan for turning over your request or desires to your spirit.

31. Imagine the end desired and feel its reality. Follow it through, and you will get definite results.

32. Decide what belief is. Know that **belief** is a **thought** in your mind and that what you think you **procreate**.

33. It is foolish to believe in sickness or anything that will hurt or harm you. Believe in perfect health, prosperity, peace, wealth and divine guidance.

34. Great and noble thoughts upon which you habitual dwell become great acts.

35. Apply the power of prayer therapy in your life. Choose a certain plan, idea, or mental picture. Unite mentally and emotionally with that idea. As you remain faithful to your mental attitude your prayer will be answered.

36. Know that you can remake yourself by giving a new blueprint to your **Spirit**.

37. The tendency of your **Spirit** is always lifeward. Your job is with your conscious mind. Feed your **Spirit** with promises that are true. Spirit is always **reproducing** according to your habitual mental patterns.

38. You build a new body every eleven months. Change your body by changing your thoughts and keeping them changed.

39. It is normal to be healthy. It is abnormal to be ill (Matthew 8:17).

40. Thoughts of jealousy, fear, worry, and anxiety tear down and destroy your nerves and glands, bringing about mental and physical diseases of all kinds.

41. Your Human Spirit is a recording machine that reproduces your habitual thinking. Think good of others, and you are actually thinking good about yourself.

42. A hateful or resentful thought is a mental poison. Do not think ill of another for to do so is to think ill of yourself. You are the only thinker in your world, and your thoughts are creative.

43. Your **Mind** is a **creative** medium; therefore, what you think and feel about the other, you are bringing to pass in your own experience. This is the **psychological** meaning of the **golden rule**. As you would that others should think about you, think you about them in the same manner.

44. To cheat, rob or defraud another brings lack, loss, and limitation to yourself. Your spirit records your inner motivations, thoughts, and feelings. When these are negative, loss, limitation and trouble come to you in countless ways. What you do to the other, you are doing to yourself.

45. Wish for the other what you wish for yourself. This is the key to **harmonious** human relations.

46. God never sends disease, sickness, accident, or suffering. We bring these things on ourselves by our own negative destructive thinking, based upon the law "as we sow, so shall we reap."

47. Your concept of **God** is the most important thing in your Life. If you really believe in a God of Love, your Human Spirit will respond by bringing countless blessings to you. Believe in the God of **Love**.

48. If a person criticizes you, and these faults are within you, rejoice, give thanks, and appreciate the comments. This gives you the opportunity to correct the particular fault.

49. You cannot be hurt by criticism when you know that you are the **master** of your thoughts, reactions, and emotions. This gives you the opportunity to pray for and bless the person, thereby blessing yourself.

50. Do the thing you are afraid to do, and the death of fear is certain. If you say to yourself with perfect confidence and faith, "I am going to master this fear", you will. Fear is a negative thought (stronghold) in your mind.

51. Your **Spirit** never sleeps. It is always on the job. It controls all your vital functions. Ask God for forgiveness, forgive yourself and everyone else before you go to sleep and healing will take place much more rapidly.

52. Guidance is given to you while you are **asleep**, sometimes in a **dream**. The **healing** currents are also **released**, and in the morning you feel refreshed and rejuvenated.

53. When troubled by the vexations and strife of the day, still the wheels of your mind and think about the wisdom intelligence lodged in your spirit, which is ready to respond to you. This will give you peace, strength, and confidence.

54. Sleep is essential for peace of mind and health of the body. Lack of sleep can cause irritation, depression and mental disorders. You need eight hours of sleep daily.

55. You are **spiritually recharged** during sleep. Adequate sleep is essential for joy and vitality in life.

56. Your **future** is in your **Mind** now, based on your habitual thinking and beliefs.

57. Give thanks for all your blessings several times a day. Furthermore, pray for the peace, happiness, and prosperity of the members of your family, your friends and all people everywhere.

58. You must sincerely desire to be happy. Nothing is accomplished without a **desire**. Desire is a **wish** with **wings** of **imagination** and **faith**. Imagine the fulfillment of your desires; feel its reality and it will come to pass. Happiness comes in answered prayers.

59. When you open your eyes in the morning say to yourself, "I choose life this day, I choose happiness today, I choose success today. I choose right action today. I choose love and goodwill for all today. I choose peace today." Pour life, love, and interest into this confession, and you have chosen happiness.

60. Fear is a person's greatest enemy. It is be- hind failure, sickness, and bad human relations. Love casts out fear. Love is an emotional attachment to the good things in life. Fall in love with honesty, integrity, justice, goodwill, and success. Live in the joyous expectancy of the best, and in- variably the best will come to you.

61. The solution lies within the problem. God re-ponds to you as you call upon Him with faith and confidence.

62. **Habit** is the function of your **Human Spirit**. There is no greater evidence of the marvelous power of your spirit, than the force and sway habit holds in your life. You are a creature of habit.

63. You form habit patterns in your Spirit by repeating a thought or act over and over until you establish tracks in your spirit and become automatic.

64. You have freedom to choose. You can choose a good habit or a bad habit. Prayer is a good habit.

65. Whatever mental picture, backed by faith; you behold in your conscious mind; your spirit will bring it to pass.

66. The only obstacle to your success and achievement is your own thought or mental image.

67. The solution lies within the problem. The answer is in every question. God responds to you as you call upon Him with Faith and confidence.

68. The only jinx that follows anyone is a fear thought repeated over and over in the mind. Break the jinx by knowing that whatever you start you will bring to a conclusion in divine order. Picture the happy ending and sustain it with confidence.

69. Your **Conscious Mind** is the **camera**, and your **spirit** is the **sensitive plate** on which you register or impress the picture.

70. To form a new habit, you must be convinced that it is desirable. When your desire to give up the bad habit is greater than your desire to continue, you are already fifty-one percent healed.

71. The statements of others cannot hurt you except through your own thoughts and mental participation. Identify yourself with your aim, which is peace, harmony, and joy. You are the only thinker in your universe.

72. When fear knocks at the door of your mind, let faith in God and all things good open the door.

73. God is no respecter of persons. God shows no favoritism. God seems to favor you once you begin to align yourself with the principles of harmony, health, joy, and peace.

74. William James said that the greatest discovery of the nineteenth century was the power of the Human Spirit touched by faith.

75. This is tremendous **power within** you. Happiness will come to you when you acquire a sublime confidence in this power. Then you will make your dreams come true.

76. Your desire is your prayer. Picture the fulfillment of your desire now and feel it's reality (Mark 11:24) and you will experience the joy of the answered prayer.

77. You must choose happiness. Happiness is a habit. It is a good habit on which to ponder often. *"Whatsoever things are true, whatsoever things are honest, whatsoever things are just, whatsoever things are pure, whatsoever things are lovely, whatsoever things are of good report; if there be any virtue, and if there be any praise, think on these things" (Philippians 4:8).*

78. There is no block to your happiness. External things are not causative. They are effect, not causes. Take your cue from the only creative principle within you. Your thoughts are the cause, and a new cause produces a new effect. Choose happiness.

79. Ignorance of mental and spiritual laws is the cause of all marital unhappiness. By praying scientifically together, you stay together.

80. You must build into your mentality the mental equivalent of what you want in a marriage partner. If you want to attract an honest, sincere and loving partner in life, you must be honest, sincere, and loving yourself.

81. Do not wonder how, why, or where you will meet the mate you are praying for, but trust implicitly the wisdom of your spirit. It has the power to carry out its mission. You do not have to assist it.

82. The happiest person is the one who brings forth the highest and the best in himself or herself. God is the highest and the best in him or her for the kingdom of God is within.

83. Feel the joy and restfulness in foreseeing the certain accomplishment of your desire. Any mental picture you have in your mind is the substance of things hoped for and the evidence of things not seen.

84. A **mental picture** is worth **a thousand words**. Your spirit will bring to pass any picture held in the mind backed by faith.

85. Remember that the **thankful heart** is always close to the riches of the kingdom of God.

86. **Mental coercion** or too much effort show anxiety and fear that block your answer – easy does it.

87. When your mind is relaxed and you accept an idea, your spirit goes to work to execute the idea.

88. Think and plan independently of traditional methods. Know that there is always an answer and a solution to every problem.

89. The feeling of health produces health; the feeling of wealth produces wealth. How do you feel?

90. **Imagination** is your most **powerful faculty**. Imagine what is lovely and of good report. You are what you imagine yourself to be.

91. Decide to be **wealthy** the easy way, with the **infallible** aid of your **Human Spirit**.

92. Trying to accumulate wealth by the sweat of your brow and hard labor is one way to become the richest man in the graveyard. You do not have to strive or slave hard.

93. **Wealth is a Human Spirit conviction**. Build into your mentality the idea of wealth.

94. **Repeat** the word **"wealth"** to yourself slowly and quietly for about five minutes prior to sleep and your spirit will bring **wealth** to pass in your experience.

95. The trouble with most people is that they have no **invisible** means of **support**.

96. The **feeling** of **wealth** produces **wealth**. Keep this in mind at all times.

97. You can overcome any mental conflict regarding wealth by affirming frequently "by day and by night I am being prospered in all of my interests."

98. Stop writing blank checks, such as, "there is not enough to go around" or "there is a shortage," and so forth. Such statements magnify and multi-ply your loss.

99. Deposit thoughts of prosperity, wealth, and success in your spirit and your spirit will give you compound interest.

100.   Envy and jealousy are stumbling blocks to the flow of wealth. Rejoice in the prosperity of others. The block of wealth is in your own mind. Destroy that block now by getting on good mental terms with everyone.

But thou shalt remember the LORD thy God: for it is he that giveth thee power to get wealth, that he may establish his covenant which he sware unto thy fathers, as it is this day.

Deuteronomy 8:18

For ye know the grace of our Lord Jesus Christ, that, though he was rich, yet for your sakes he became poor, that ye through his poverty might be rich.

II Corinthians 8:9

Made in the USA
Middletown, DE
25 April 2022